The
PRINCIPAL OFFICERS
A Practical Guide

The
PRINCIPAL
OFFICERS
A Practical Guide

Richard Johnson

Lewis Masonic

The Principal Officers – A Practical Guide is a
companion volume to the author's previous book
The Assistant Officers – A Practical Guide, also
published by Lewis Masonic (2002).

Front cover:
*The Principal Officers' chairs in
Cambridge Masonic Hall*

First published 2003

ISBN 0 85318 120 9

Published by Lewis Masonic

an imprint of Ian Allan Publishing
Hersham, Surrey KT12 4RG.
Printed by Ian Allan Printing Ltd,
Horsham, Surrey KT12 4RH

Contents

Preface

This book is written to guide the Principal Officers of a lodge, the three senior regular Officers, through the range of duties that they will be expected to perform during their year of office. Often these positions are filled by Masons who have worked their way through the ranks of the junior offices, but even so some explanatory information may be of use to them in comprehending the instructions contained in their lodge rituals. This book amplifies aspects of the basic ceremonial to be performed within the lodge, explaining in some instances why certain actions are required at different times in the ritual, and outlines some of the additional duties that may be expected of these Officers. But above all it is written to help ensure that the Mason is prepared for the range of duties annexed to each office as he embarks on his final steps towards and into the Chair of his lodge.

This book is not written as an exhaustive guide to every possible variation that exists in the Craft ritual across the over 7,000 lodges that operate within the English Constitution. This would be an unnecessarily repetitious method of explaining the duties of each office. It is recognised that each lodge has its own traditions, some retained for over two centuries of working and some couched in a language specific to that lodge, and no Director of Ceremonies wants any member of his lodge trying to adopt new concepts that are foreign to its individual modus operandi. Again this book should be read in conjunction with the lodge ritual, and only as a basis for general reference has the Emulation ritual been alluded to in each section of the book, because it is widely available. Among the other rituals adopted by some lodges are Logic, Oxford, Perfect, Revised, Stability, Sussex, Taylor's, West End, the Craft Guide and the Complete Workings. Still further rituals exist in the Bristol lodges, and also in Shakspere Lodge (East Lancashire) and Pellipar Lodge (Cartwright's).

Even in these exhaustive rituals there are times when the ritual book does not indicate how a certain action is performed or if any words are used. Each lodge will have adopted a stratagem for coping with these apparent blanks, and any Officer is recommended to check with his Director or Assistant Director of Ceremonies if he needs any guidance to ensure that he maintains the lodge traditions. In other cases the methodology of the 'standard' ritual has had to be slightly revised because of the geography of the lodge room or the furniture contained therein. As a senior Officer of the lodge the Principal Officer will have been attending the practice meetings regularly, and will have already learned of the usefulness of going through the detail of what is required at a lodge meeting and when, where and how it should be enacted. In this way the lodge traditions are already being inculcated into the Mason, so that he has developed a feel for how his lodge ritual flows, and generally formed an impression as to why the ritual proceeds as it does.

Having noted the preceding, this book is written to give the Principal Officers an added degree of confidence about their work and their roles in the lodge. It is further hoped that this will help the Officer to enjoy his Masonry more, and indeed there is very little value belonging to an organisation in which you do not enjoy participating. However, as many experienced Masons have found previously, the degree of confidence and enjoyment in carrying out any role in the lodge is greatly increased by making sure you are as prepared as possible for the work. The adage 'practice makes perfect' is still as valid as before, and without practising you may not be able to perform your prescribed duties with as much satisfaction to yourself and to your lodge as you might otherwise be capable of doing.

Introduction

How many Principal Officers are there in the lodge?' These are the words spoken at the start of every lodge meeting, addressed by the Master to the Junior Warden. In reply the Master himself is mentioned, along with Senior and Junior Wardens, and later on that they are placed in the East, West and South of the lodge room respectively. It is interesting how often in Freemasonry the work is divided into threes: three junior floor Officers, three degree ceremonies, three Principals in Royal Arch, etc. So it should not come as any surprise that the Craft lodge is ruled by three, as noted in the explanation of the second degree tracing board.

In this book the work of the Principal Officers is laid out in the form of doing the routine things first and then the special things last. In this sense the installation is seen as special and is covered at the end of each section, more as a hand-over from your current duties and then being invested into your next office, because you may have 11 routine lodge meetings but only one installation meeting each year. In the olden times lodges sometimes held installations every six months and some of them would meet every two weeks, so they would still have seen the installation as a special event, and as an aside it is little wonder that the Secretary's minutes tended towards brevity rather than the reverse. After the installation section the other duties of the Officers, both within and outside the lodge room, are also noted, so it will be beneficial for an inquiring brother to read the whole of each chapter at a time in order to gain an appraisal of all the work that might arise for that Officer. Even then there may be more detail about certain procedures contained in one chapter than in the others, so as to avoid being unnecessarily repetitious throughout the book, and at least a cursory perusal of the other chapters is also to be recommended.

The other post covered in this book is that of Immediate Past Master. Being seated immediately to the left of the Master, the latter can benefit from the advice and assistance able to be given by the previous incumbent. Whilst the Immediate Past Master is not an Officer of the lodge, the new Master will be particularly grateful for gentle and timely guidance with regard to his duties as he begins to operate in his new role in the lodge. The Immediate Past Master is expected to step back into the Chair of King Solomon if for some reason the Master is unable to be present at a meeting, and many have found in their year after the Chair that they are still going through every word of the ritual in case the Master should require assistance at any time.

Principal Officers' Pedestals

The Principal Officers' pedestals of Cestrian Lodge, No 425 of Chester. The lodge records show that a Master's pedestal was donated to the lodge in 1839, and one of the pedestals appears in a lodge caricature dated 1842, so they may be derived from the first items of furniture used by the lodge. The pictures show the Junior Warden's (above left), Senior Warden's (above right) and Master's (left) pedestals. The Junior Warden's pedestal (oppposite) in the Cambridge lodge room, is one of a set of three belonging to Cantabrigia Lodge, No 3532.

10

The Wardens

It is obvious to even the newly admitted Entered Apprentice that in the lodge room there are three Officers set apart from the rest. They are each seated in an imposing and elevated seat and behind an equally imposing pedestal, usually with a large free-standing candleholder alongside. At certain times in the proceedings these three interact together while the other brethren either stand to order or sit and listen, which immediately marks them as occupying different and pre-eminent roles in the lodge.

At the investiture of the Officers at an installation meeting, the format of words used for the Wardens is different from those for the other members.

The Master says, 'I appoint you as *my* Senior/Junior Warden, and I invest you with the *insignia* (not jewel) of your office.' In fact traditionally the appointment of the Wardens was the Master's personal choice, even though nowadays in many lodges there is usually a standard progression to the Chair of King Solomon through the junior and then the senior positions in the lodge. Occasionally, however, a member of the lodge can be accelerated through the ranks to be appointed a Warden at the request of the Master, although the latter would be advised to have confirmed the agreement and support of at least the senior Past Masters of the lodge before so doing.

11

The Master and the Wardens combine to open and close every lodge meeting, and also in moving the operations of the lodge up into or down from the second and third degrees, whether by virtue or in full. In some lodges the Wardens will propose and second many of the formal resolutions required by the Master to be put to the lodge, as well as requesting the confirmation of the minutes of the previous meeting if the Secretary has recorded them accurately. The Wardens may also be required to countersign the minute book for the Secretary along with the Master, and they may also be the prime movers in proposing other brethren to additional duties, such as representatives on various committees and as auditors. They thus occupy the role of 'right-hand men' for the Master, and in formal processions around the lodge room they will closely accompany him, normally preceding him into the room and following immediately after him when going out of the room.

In many lodges, whenever the Master is unable to be present, the Immediate Past Master will occupy the Master's chair, or another Past Master can do so, and he will open and close the lodge in his stead. The importance of the Wardens is underlined in other Constitutions, because in the Master's absence it is they who open the lodge. The opening ritual is obviously modified to accommodate the necessarily different method of performing the catechism of the question and answer session at the start of the meeting, but it is the Senior Warden who will formally open the lodge. If both the Master and the Senior Warden are unavoidably absent, then it is the Junior Warden who does so, and it is an interesting mental exercise to think through how the opening is altered. If the Master were to be absent for an extended period of time, whether through work or illness, then it would also be the Senior Warden who would summon the lodge to meet at the appropriate time and place, although in these days of global communications the Master should be able to keep in touch with his lodge from wherever he is. It is also a confirmation of how important the position of Warden was in the early days of Freemasonry, and obviously still is in certain locations around the world.

In meetings when a degree is being conferred, the candidates are presented to all three Principal Officers, who each have different roles to play in the ceremonies. To the alert Mason who has recently been appointed to be a Warden, there will be a slight feeling of *déjà vu*. Whilst operating as a Deacon, you will have guided the candidate through the colloquies with the Wardens, and in order to formulate the response for the candidate you will have had to listen to the questions put by each Warden in turn. In this sense you will have already done much of the spadework, as you are now merely re-enacting the colloquies from the other side of the pairing. You will also have additional parts of the ritual to undertake where there are no interactions with the Deacons, but these tend to be not pieces at different stages of the

12

ceremony, rather than being almost constantly in action as the Deacons are.

In a similar sense the interactions that the Wardens have with the Master, at the opening and closing, etc., is also useful training for when you occupy the Chair of King Solomon. In the second degree it is pointed out to the candidate that Masonry is a progressive science, and the progression from Inner Guard to Master (if that is the route adopted by your lodge) usefully builds sequentially between each successive office. Even for people who do not feel they are particularly suited to learning by rote, this gradual accumulation of knowledge serves gently to build up confidence so that the final culmination of their career in the Chair of the lodge is not as traumatic as might otherwise have been thought. Interestingly it also underlines the usefulness if not the need for you to occupy each of the lodge offices in turn, so that you do not make too large a progressive leap up the ladder that may leave you feeling out of your depth — some people can cope with this, but many will prefer not to have to.

Additionally as you sit back in your elevated seat in the lodge room, you can observe with a slightly more dispassionate eye how the overall ceremony is proceeding, which may tempt you one day to try your hand as Director of Ceremonies or his Assistant. You will certainly be able to discern that the ritual is made up of many component parts which neatly dovetail into one another, and the efficient transition between one part and the next will help to ensure that each ceremony flows smoothly towards a successful conclusion.

The Junior Warden

A t the installation the Junior Warden is informed that he is to assist the Master and Senior Warden in controlling the lodge, to ensure that all visitors are known or proved, and to assume charge of all matters concerning refreshment for and of the brethren.

An Outline of the Duties – Old and New

Dealing with the last first, the words used are 'ostensible Steward of the lodge', and is a reference to the many duties that the Junior Warden used to undertake in the early lodges, normally in conjunction with the Tyler. This was in the days before the Inner Guard was a regular Officer in the lodge, although in some ways the Junior Warden, Inner Guard and Tyler still work as a team formally to admit brethren and candidates through the door of the lodge room once it is in session.

Whereas at one time the Junior Warden collected the dining fees from members and visitors, the lodge Treasurer usually performs this task. Sometimes he deputes the lodge Stewards to assist in the manual collection of monies, and often also to sell raffle tickets and other items for charitable purposes to assist the Charity Steward. In this sense the larger number of current lodge offices from the early days of a 'perfect lodge' of seven or more has been of greatest benefit to the Junior Warden, and the several Stewards of the lodge are now used to remove many of these former duties from him. The Junior Warden would also previously have liaised with the Tyler in looking after the lodge finances, as the former was responsible for paying for the meals and the latter was responsible for collecting subscriptions — often on a meeting-by-meeting basis, in the days before lodge Treasurers were appointed to oversee both aspects of the lodge finances. All that traditionally remains for the Junior Warden at the festive board is proposing the toast to the visitors, although in some lodges even this duty is shared out among the members.

With regard to controlling the lodge, you will already be aware that the Wardens answer the Master's knocks with the gavel by the use of their own

14

gavels, in opening or closing the lodge in any degree and also for calling the attention of the brethren to the next item of business. As the Principal Officers are positioned strategically around the lodge room, there should be little excuse for any brother to be continuing a conversation once the three knocks for attention have been sounded, so make sure your own use of the gavel is clearly audible. In some lodges the Wardens stand with the Master after sounding their gavels, for example at the 'risings' when the meeting is coming to a conclusion. If your lodge is one that does so, then remember on which occasions you stand and on which you remain seated — it does not look well-practised for one Warden to be seated while the other is standing, and a tentative and uncertain half-crouching attitude looks even worse. These are apparently minor points, but they show you understand your new role from the time you are invested into it, and you will be called on to perform all of those duties during the remainder of the installation meeting and banquet, except that hopefully any latecomers have already arrived or given up. Although one of your first duties after investiture will be to assist in closing the lodge rather than opening it, it is perhaps more helpful for general reference that the summary of your formal duties begins as a normal lodge meeting will do.

Opening and Closing and the General Business of the Lodge

You have seen the opening and closing of the lodge on many, many occasions, and perhaps frequently mentally dozed through it because in many lodges it only involves the Principal Officers, with minor interruptions from the Inner Guard and Immediate Past Master. In other lodges every floor Officer inside the room (Inner Guard to Senior Warden) will answer personally with regard to his particular duties. But you have probably not paid too much attention to the words spoken to the Master by the Wardens, and now you are going to have to do so.

Your lodge may process into the lodge room, and some lodges invite visiting Masters and Provincial Officers to join in the procession. This will halt and turn inwards so that the Master can make his way between the two rows of people to his chair. Regardless of the length of the procession, your place will be immediately behind or more usually in front of the Master of your own lodge, alongside the Senior Warden, who will probably be to your right and therefore on the inside of the procession as it sweeps round the eastern side of the lodge room. Apart from indicating seniority, as you are second Principal Officer to peel off the shorter procession proceeding to the West, it means you do not have to cross the Senior Warden to do so.

The first words of the opening ceremony are fired at the Junior Warden, who is normally named because the lodge is not yet open. Technically,

15

therefore, you should only answer without using the title 'Master', though some lodges seem not to mind, and then you should name the Inner Guard rather than use his title. Your response to the Master that all is well may or may not be preceded by a knock, and after the first Master-to-Senior Warden exchange it is the Master and not you that calls the brethren to order as Masons. You then begin the process of working your way up through the list of floor Officers. As stated above, you may answer on behalf of the other Officers until it is your turn or your lodge may prefer to make everyone take part and, after you have answered the Master's and Senior Warden's knocks to open the lodge, you adjust the column of your office accordingly. After joining in an opening ode if it were not sung beforehand, you can sit down. In some lodges the candles are formally lit after the opening, an operation which the Deacons or a Steward will perform; in others the candles will all be lit before the meeting starts; while in many modern lodges there are electric lights which you or the Deacons will switch on at the appropriate time.

For each item of business you will assist the Master if he knocks for attention, and stand with him if that is the lodge protocol. In some lodges you may have to formally second the Senior Warden's proposition that the minutes of the previous regular lodge meeting have been recorded satisfactorily by the Secretary, and you may be required to sign them in confirmation. If the latter is the case, the Deacons or even the Secretary will bring the minute book to you.

Opening in the second and third degrees is a little different from the first degree. Now the Master asks you to prove the brethren are entitled to stay in the lodge room in the higher degree, and this is in accordance with your duties explained at the installation that you will examine visitors; your own lodge members you should already know. This will be the first time that you have not come to order with the rest of the brethren, but you have to remain in the stance of the lower degree so that you can report the satisfactory proofs the brethren have given. The knocks from the Master through to the Inner Guard are principally to inform the Tyler that you are now in a higher degree — everyone in the lodge room should be aware of that fact already. If you know that there are visitors from another Constitution present, then their signs may differ from the ones you usually see, and if you are concerned about what to expect, then ask the member who has invited them to go through their signs, with or without the visitors in attendance, so that you are forewarned.

The only difference between the second and the third degree opening is that the latter has several additional questions for both Wardens, but the general scope is the same. In the closing from the third degree there is a great deal more activity than in the others, and you have to demonstrate the signs of the three degrees quietly to your brother Senior Warden. The exact position in the lodge room where this will be done and how you arrive there will have been practised by you and him beforehand under the watchful eye of the Director of Ceremonies, because this is a sort of revision or demonstration class for all the members of your lodge. You should remember exactly what the signs should be — some lodges include the pass grips and words, and others do not, but normally you arrive and depart from the appointed place holding the third degree sign.

In the final closing from the third degree you only check that the lodge is properly guarded, and you then answer the Senior Warden's knocks according to the lodge's custom; in some cases the Senior Warden has closed the lodge and used the second degree knocks, and in others he has repeated the third degree knocks of the Master. Whichever is the case, you should ideally use the second degree knocks, as you are confirming the closure of the lodge from the higher degree, but more especially the knocks are your instruction to the Inner Guard as to how he should communicate to the Tyler. This is the only way the Tyler knows in what degree the lodge is currently operating, and for you and the Inner Guard to repeat the third degree knocks would be somewhat misleading for the Outer Guard, but each lodge has its own traditions.

Closing in full from the second degree is much simpler; two additional questions and answers are required of you and also a different final set of words from the other two degrees, which you will happily remember to add. Again take care which knocks you are to give so that the Tyler knows what is going on. And closing by virtue from both degrees is even simpler — the Master says all that is required and delivers the knocks of the lower degree himself, and you merely answer the Senior Warden's knocks for the Inner Guard to pick up.

Towards the end of the meeting there are the 'risings', when the Master rises to ask if any Grand Lodge, Provincial Grand Lodge, or general communications have been received; possibly the Wardens stand as well or you may only need to answer the Master's knock for attention. And then, as in the opening, you are the first to respond with regard to duties when closing the lodge, but you can now address the Inner Guard by his title, after which you may use one or three knocks before replying to the Master, addressing him as such because the lodge is in formal session. After the Senior Warden has closed the lodge, you then confirm its closure and warn the brethren when the next meeting will be, adjust your column of office to confirm the lodge is at refreshment and extinguish the candle or electric light if required. You might note that technically the lodge should never be unsupervised by either

Warden, so your column should be raised promptly before the Senior Warden's is lowered, not as detailed in the standard ritual books, but most people have their minds on the meal at this stage of the proceedings and possibly will not notice. Another word of warning: different lodges expect different knocks from the Wardens. Some retain the first degree knocks for all Officers; some expect the Senior Warden to close the lodge, as instructed by the Master, by fewer knocks than the Master and which you repeat; and others expect you to be the first with fewer knocks, so be aware of what your lodge traditions require.

If a procession was formed to conduct you to your pedestal, then in all probability on retiring another one will pick you up, followed by the Senior Warden and then the Master, after which you remain standing while the Director of Ceremonies organises the rest of the retiring procession to include dignitaries as required. Even in lodges where the Principal Officers are seated in place for the start of the meeting, a retiring procession may be formed to facilitate their departure. Outside the lodge room door you and the other Principal Officers may be expected to greet all of the visitors as they file out after you, a nice courtesy which takes very little time and emphasises or reaffirms the friendly welcome they hopefully received when they arrived. In any case, you are the ostensible Steward of the lodge whilst at refreshment, so it is an opportunity for any visitor to ask for clarification about dining, etc., which he may not be able to do as easily if you have immediately dived into the bar!

Latecomers, Visitors and Candidates
In the examination of visiting brethren, different lodges adopt different strategies. Many lodges do not ensure visitors are formally vouched for prior to entering the lodge room before the start of a meeting, perhaps assuming that they are all invitees of one member or another, or that they will themselves volunteer that they are strangers. In any case, when the brethren are called to order it will be obvious if someone does not know what he is doing, although you should be warned that Masons from different Constitutions often have different signs by which to prove themselves. Some lodges insist on asking at the start of their meetings if every visitor is vouched for, to comply with the recommendation in the Book of Constitutions, others will only admit visitors once the lodge has opened, and then a member has to stand up and personally vouch for each visitor. If no-one does so, or if a visitor arrives late and unexpectedly to a meeting and is not known within, then some action is required. The Junior Warden should leave the lodge room to prove the visitor, up to the highest degree to be worked during the meeting, and also to see his Grand Lodge certificate and letter of good standing from

18

his lodge. Some lodges will request the Director of Ceremonies to do so, and others — especially with a Past Master outside the door of the lodge — will ask the Tyler to prove the visitor before he reports that a brother requests admission. This latter approach is certainly an efficient way of conducting the examination, but the ultimate responsibility still rests with the Junior Warden, so you have been warned.

The problem is much easier with your own lodge members if they are late and candidates when they enter the lodge. With the latter, the dialogues with the Inner Guard and then Master are detailed in the formal ritual, and with the former they should be known personally by you anyway. Whoever wants to enter the lodge, it may be the protocol in your lodge for you to repeat whatever the Inner Guard announces, when you will be fervently hoping there is only one person with an easily recognisable rank, otherwise you may need an incredible short-term memory. Your lodge may require the Inner Guard to address the Master directly at once, but if you are to request the Inner Guard to direct his announcement to the Master, try to use the usual words, otherwise the Inner Guard may be confused — especially if he is new to the job. As with any part of the business or ritual, the lodge has its own conventions with regard to the forms of words to be used, and the meeting flows smoothly if the right words are spoken at the right times.

The ceiling rose in the Chester lodge room, from which is suspended the central chandelier, making a stylish 'blazing star, or glory in the centre'.

19

The Degree Ceremonies

As a precursor to the Wardens' duties in the three degree ceremonies, it is worth analysing the different parts of the ritual contained therein. The three ceremonies are variations on a theme, and for the temporarily unthinking it is relatively easy to transpose from one into another. In order to remember exactly what you need to do in each and when, it is worthwhile breaking down the format into its constituent parts. The initiation begins differently from the other degrees, because a non-Mason is being inducted for the first time, but the basic parts of the ceremonies all fall into four distinct sections: the presentation, obligation, investiture and explanation, which are amplified as follows:

PRESENTATION (differs between the first and the other degrees)

First degree:
Introduction — the candidate enters the lodge and kneels for prayer.
Presentation — the Master announces that the candidate is making a circuit of the lodge in order to be inspected and introduced formally to the Wardens, after which the Senior Warden presents the candidate to the Master.

Second and third degrees:
Introduction — the Master introduces and tests the candidate verbally on the knowledge he gained from the previous degree ceremony.
Entrusting (test of merit) — the candidate is given the pass grip and password in order to re-enter the lodge in a higher degree, and he retires to be prepared physically.
Presentation — the candidate re-enters and makes one or two circuits of the lodge, communicating the signs, tokens and words of the first degree (to the Junior Warden) and second degree (to the Senior Warden) as appropriate. The Master then announces that the candidate is making his final circuit of the lodge, in order to communicate the test of merit to the Senior Warden, after which the latter presents the candidate to the Master.

Standard to all degrees:

OBLIGATION

Obligation — the Deacon guides the candidate correctly to the East, who then takes and seals his obligation, and the symbolism of the Great and Lesser Lights is explained in the first degree; in the third degree there is an additional extensive section on the symbolism of death.

20

INVESTITURE

Entrusting (signs) — the candidate is shown the signs, tokens and words, the last two being repeated with the Deacon (only with the Master in the third degree).

Demonstration — the candidate is presented to the Wardens to practise and display his new information (not in the third degree).

Investiture — of the new apron, usually by the Senior Warden; followed by appropriate remarks on what the new role entails, including an extensive description of charity in the first degree.

EXPLANATION

Working tools — their symbolism is explained (follows the traditional history in the third degree).

Charge — although the first degree charge is always delivered, the charges after the other ceremonies are delivered less frequently.

Tracing Board — the second and third degree tracing boards are usually delivered in the ceremony (the third is in the traditional history) rather than the charge, whilst in the first degree the tracing board, which contains a wealth of information of great interest to a newcomer, is more rarely delivered.

Questions and Answers — in some lodges at the end of the first or second degree, the candidate is shown a rehearsal of the answers he will need to learn before presenting himself for the next degree.

It can be seen that the second and third degrees add an entrusting between the introduction and the presentation, and an entrusting is always followed by a demonstration by the candidate of his previous and/or new knowledge. The Senior Warden is always the one who tests the candidate on the pass grip and password he has been given previously by the Master. This demonstration of new knowledge is also seen after the obligation, when the candidate communicates what the Master has taught him and both of the Wardens test him in turn, with the Senior Warden being more detailed in his questioning (except this is not called for in the third degree).

   The rule of thumb is that the total number of circuits made by the candidate equals the degree being conferred. In the first degree the Junior Deacon has only one circuit to perform with the candidate, and he will wait for the Master's announcement before starting. The Senior Deacon has two circuits in total for a second degree and three for a third, and he too awaits the Master's announcement before starting the final lap. The main job of the

Deacons is to ensure that the candidate is placed at the correct position for the next part of the ceremony. Up until the candidate being invested with his apron the format is generally common to almost all lodges, but the remaining items will vary from lodge to lodge, depending on how the lodge organises the delivery of those later items in the ceremony.

In all of the ceremonies, as Junior Warden you are the first Principal Officer to whom any candidate is introduced. This is as it should be, because at the installation you were charged with investigating all those entering the lodge, and you should halt any further progress they might attempt to make if all is not well. Your first job, therefore, when the candidate enters the lodge is to check he is properly attired; although the Inner Guard should have checked the Tyler's work, you are the guardian of the lodge and actually supervise the Inner Guard and Tyler in ensuring that all those entering do so correctly. In the second and third degree ceremonies you are also delegated to check that the candidates know the correct signs and words of their current and previous degrees, again part of confirming they have a legitimate right to be there. It may seem a little over the top, as you will know the candidates because they are lodge members, but at least it has the merit of making for consistency in the formalities of the lodge workings.

You are also the first of the Principal Officers to check that the candidate has absorbed the information given him during the course of the ceremony. In this sense you are acting as a formal gatekeeper for the Senior Warden and his more detailed questioning, even though he has just seen the ceremony for himself, which again is a consistent approach. And then when the candidate has retired to redress himself, it is you as Junior Warden who permits him to re-enter the lodge room, or who requests the Master to do so.

First Degree

Perhaps more so than in any other degree, it is a courtesy to introduce yourself to the candidate for initiation prior to the ceremony. You may well have seen him at the interview he undertook before being recommended to the lodge for membership, but remember he will be blindfolded, and his being able to recognise a friendly voice early in the ceremony will give him the additional confidence that he is among friends. You do not have to reveal much about the coming ceremony, but you might mention that he will be introduced by the Junior Deacon to you as one of the Principal Officers at different times during the ceremony. If you are delegated to deliver the charge after initiation, you might add that there is a set piece of ritual that he will have to listen to, but which will help to put his mind at ease if he has any residual doubts about the demands of Freemasonry in comparison with his other duties in life. Whilst the detail of what is to happen should be properly revealed during the

22

ceremony, it will enable the candidate to pick up one or two frames of reference to help him through the evening.

As the candidate is about to enter, the Inner Guard will first inform you that someone wants to enter the lodge room, and you either ask him directly to find out who it is, or you report to the Master for him to tell you to do so. The latter seems a little laborious, but your lodge has doubtless enjoyed many years with that protocol, and would prefer to enjoy many more years of the same. With it being a non-Mason seeking admission, only the Master can approve his entrance, but you should check he is properly prepared for the ceremony as soon as he steps through the doorway. The Master will then question the candidate and call for prayer, after which the Junior Deacon will lead the candidate round the lodge room to your pedestal.

The Deacon is required to make the candidate's hand strike your shoulder three times. Different lodges perform this action in different ways; in some the candidate is led to the East side of the pedestal to come quite close to you, in others he will be presented from the front of the pedestal. Either way, and especially in the latter, you are required to lean towards the candidate so your shoulder comes within easy range of his arm-span. Remember too that your seat is normally somewhat above the lodge room floor, by being placed on a raised platform, and that the pedestal itself may also be relatively tall, so do everything you can to make the Deacon's and candidate's lives as easy as possible. After a few questions directed at the Deacon, you formally take and return the candidate's hand to his jurisdiction. Then, apart from a few answering gavel strokes to the Master's bidding, you can relax a little until he introduces his Principal Officers and their situations in the lodge room to the candidate.

After the Master has then completed entrusting the candidate with the details of the first degree sign, token and word, you are now the first lodge member to talk to the candidate after he has been entrusted, and many lodges will emphasise that your tone should be welcoming rather than being magisterial. You can also help the Junior Deacon greatly by how you pose your questions. If you start by looking the candidate in the eye, and then at the end of each question turn to the Deacon, it will be a reminder to the candidate that the Master has just told him to instruct the candidate on the answers to be given. Whilst there is no real harm in an enthusiastic candidate volunteering the answers to prove he has been taking in what has gone before, it can complicate the Junior Deacon's life and increase the pressure he will be feeling — remember that you probably once held that office previously.

You should let the Junior Deacon adjust the candidate's grip on your hand into the appropriate position, only offering to correct it if necessary, and then complete your grip on the candidate's hand. It is important that the candidate recognises the proper method, because at some time in the future when he is visiting another lodge he may be tested, and not only he but also in a sense your lodge is on trial that he was taught correctly. And finally, when you pass the candidate's hand back to the Junior Deacon, a conspiratorial smile that they have both done well will doubtless be gratefully received by each of them.

The candidate is then invested with his apron by the Senior Warden and receives the North East address, and then he may well be conducted to your pedestal, if that is where the explanation of the working tools is to be given. In other lodges the Master may himself explain their significance at his own pedestal, or your lodge might have a tradition of delivering the explanation elsewhere. If your pedestal is in use, it may be your job to explain the tools, but even if a junior or someone else is doing the work, try to go through the words with him; if you are following the words and there is a pause for assistance, it will be much more preferable and efficient coming locally from you than needing to be shouted across the room by someone else. If the juniors in your lodge are entrusted with the explanations of the tools, then you may have already done this part of the ceremony, but there is always added confidence in the mind of the brother making the explanation if he knows you are supporting him close by.

After this the candidate retires and returns, again with you or the Master permitting him to do so, and then in many lodges the charge after initiation is the prerogative of the Junior Warden at least once in his year of office. In some lodges you may be expected to deliver this standing up and in others you can remain seated, and you may have requested someone near to your pedestal to be a local prompter if you require it. With the delivery of what is a fairly long piece of prose, there is the temptation to try to rush it through. This hardly ever works, and a clearly-spoken charge is much more likely to be intelligible to the candidate, and everyone else present, than a speedy but partly garbled version.

You should remember that the candidate is struggling to take in a great deal of information that is new to him, in strange surroundings and in the presence of many people he does not yet know very well. He probably feels more comfortable now he is properly dressed, and the charge can be a useful summary of what he has been through and what he is expected to do in future. You do not make him a Mason on the night of initiation; if he were indeed first prepared in his heart, then he already had many of the characteristics of a Mason, and Freemasonry supplies the framework upon which to refine and develop those essential characteristics. Thus a calmly delivered and clearly enunciated charge can give him practical guidance on how to view the different facets of Freemasonry, and help him logically to begin to put into context all that has happened during the evening.

The charge, when the candidate reads it later, should allay any remaining worries he may have about the organisation he is joining. Some lodges actually present a written copy of the charge to the candidate after the ceremony, as in all probability he will not remember a great deal of it at the time, and they explain to him that the charge is one of the pieces of Masonic ritual that can be shown to family and friends if it would be helpful. It would be gratifying if the candidate were able to recall parts of your presentation as he reads the charge in the peace and quiet of his home, and there will always be some parts that he has especially noted during its delivery — even from the hurried ones. Thereafter you can relax, because your duties for this ceremony are over.

Second Degree

The second degree ceremony usually begins with the Junior Deacon collecting the candidate and then the Master questioning the candidate about his knowledge of his current degree status. Then follows an entrusting by the Master of the pass grip and password for the candidate to be able to re-enter the lodge room for the passing. In this preliminary part of the ceremony the Wardens play no role, and after the candidate has retired from the lodge, they then assist the Master to open the lodge in the higher degree. In the second degree there is another version of the exchanges between you and the Master, and you and the Inner Guard, and then you have to prove that the brethren are Fellowcrafts. This is different from opening in the first degree, when it is the Master who requests the brethren to stand to order as Masons, and your eyes should rove around the lodge room as the Brethren are proving themselves before replying to the Master. Be aware of visitors from other Constitutions (and Scotland and Ireland provide the most frequent visitors to English lodges) as their signs may at first sight seem rather unusual. If you know someone in the lodge has friends from Scotland or Ireland, then let him or them show outside the meeting what their signs are and explain them to you — it is useful Masonic research, and may be helpful for you when a visitor arrives unexpectedly at a future date. You then confirm that the brethren have proved themselves, and come to order as a Fellowcraft yourself, after which the Master follows your example and opens the lodge in the second degree.

When the Inner Guard announces the candidate wanting to gain admission with a password, either directly to the Master or through you, your first duty will be as in the first degree: to check that the candidate is properly prepared. Hopefully no action will be needed, as the Tyler and Inner Guard between them should have performed their duties as required, but if anything is amiss

25

you are still the formal custodian over all people entering the lodge once opened — be vigilant about your responsibilities.

After the prayer the candidate will start his initial perambulation, and you will be the first Principal Officer to question him, regarding what he learned during his initiation. Be prepared for a look of surprise on the candidate's face when the Senior Deacon prompts him with the full word, as the candidate has been taught over and over again never to repeat it in full, until now. A smile of encouragement at this interchange will help to calm any butterflies the candidate may be experiencing, as well as a warm handshake before he leaves you.

Thereafter the ceremony belongs to the Senior Warden and the Master, the one presenting and the other obligating and entrusting again. You are next called into action when the Senior Deacon presents the candidate to you for his first testing of his new-found information from the second degree, and as in the initiation you only assess the step, grip and word. After this the Senior Warden's pedestal may well be used for the explanation of the working tools of the degree, so you have little else further to do. When the candidate re-enters properly dressed, you may be called upon as a local prompter for the member delivering the explanation of the second degree tracing board, but otherwise your duties are completed. A word on prompting: if you know the passage fully and are confident that you can prompt accurately and immediately from memory, then every credit for being able to do so; if not, then I would seriously contemplate using a book. Either way you will need to be listening intently, but you have a perfect shield behind which to read the book without making it too noticeable, and an incorrect prompt from memory is likely to cause additional confusion in the presenter's mind, which is already racing through endless possibilities as he grinds to a halt in his presentation.

You will then have to close down to the first degree, and if you do so in full, and there is not very much to it, you have only a few extra words to remember. If you close by virtue it is even easier: the Master says all that needs to be said, and you repeat his knocks before sitting down again.

Third Degree
The preliminaries for the third degree are very similar to those of the second, except that usually it is the Senior Deacon who collects the candidate for the questions and initial entrusting. After the candidate has left the lodge room you assist the Master to open the lodge in the third degree. Again it is you who has to prove all of the brethren are entitled to stay in the lodge in this higher degree, so make it obvious that you are checking that they are all going through the correct actions. For the third degree, however, there is another

26

question and answer session between the Master and his Wardens before the opening is completed, so be prepared with the right answer to the Master's first question and the rest routinely falls into place, after which you await the return of the candidate.

As in the second degree, you are the first to prove the candidate's knowledge of the previous degree ceremonies, and again you are restricted to checking on the first degree only. The rest of the ceremony passes you by until the Wardens have to leave their chairs in order to replace the Deacons. Your lodge will have a protocol by which to enact this change, which probably includes you waiting for the Senior Warden to walk from the West until he is parallel with your pedestal, and you both walk in step to your appointed places. You may need to take with you the appropriate instrument from your pedestal for the re-enactment, or you may be using the jewel on your collar, but at the required moment you will strike the candidate, hopefully catching his hair rather than the full Monty. You and the Senior Warden assist the candidate to move and stand upright again, and then repeat the process after the Senior Warden has also struck the candidate; a stage whisper in the candidate's ear will help him understand what you are trying to make him do.

Then the Master joins in the fun, and the candidate becomes horizontal. If you are relatively small in stature you will have been hoping that during your years in the principal offices all of the candidates will be even smaller than you. However, even with a large candidate a suitable whisper in his ear will enable him to help you to alter his position, after which you correct his limbs accordingly — crossed feet and hands perhaps, and possibly covered with the sheet. The Wardens then stand either side of the candidate while the Master delivers his observations on what has been re-enacted, and you will be asked to attempt to elevate the candidate. If a sheet has been folded over him, you will need to reach under the edge to locate his hand, and then ensure there is no positive grip — possibly by holding his wrist with the other hand to prevent any further movement. You then report back to the Master, and in some lodges you step back and in others you will walk around the candidate in order to do so. You may use the first or third degree sign, as your lodge dictates, and then you probably hold the latter sign until the Senior Warden has completed a similar series of actions.

You then prepare the candidate for elevation, uncovering him if required and warning him by a whisper what you are going to do, and the three of you help him up. If the candidate is of quite a size, then let him help you as well, but try not to perform too rapid a lifting operation because that may cause the candidate to become somewhat disoriented. The final job is for the Wardens to ensure that the candidate is standing correctly with the hand stretched out accordingly — and some lodges have the arm straight out, the palm in line or at right angles, and others have a bent arm round the back of the Master. You are then requested to return to your pedestals, which you and the Senior Warden will do together until you peel off into your place while he continues to his.

All this presumes that your lodge room uses the floor for this part of the ceremony. There are some lodge rooms where a formal box or a hole in the floor are used, and obviously the re-enactment has to be modified to cope with these situations. It will also be beneficial for you to talk the candidate through this aspect of the evening, because there is no need to allow him to become unduly concerned at any time — it is only a re-enactment. In other lodges there is a formal perambulation of some Officers around the candidate whilst he is horizontal, and in one or two the lodge is called off so that the candidate can meditate at some length about the ceremony he is going through! These variations are high on the list of the enjoyable aspects of visiting other lodges, to see how they conduct their equivalent ceremonies.

With you leaving your pedestal, the format of the third degree ceremony is already different from the others, and it continues in this vein. After the Master has entrusted the candidate with his new information, the latter exits the lodge room — no apron invested, no North East or South East corner, and no working tools at this time. On his re-entrance the candidate receives the apron that will stand him in good stead until he attains the Chair of King Solomon, and he has an address from the Master which is a shorter equivalent of the corner addresses in the other degrees. He then has the third degree tracing board explained, although this takes up only a small part of the traditional history, and he finally has the working tools explained to him. In some lodges the Master performs all of the work in this degree, and Emulation expects him to do so, but in many others the Immediate Past Master or another predecessor will take over the second part of the work of the ceremony. And there is something rather satisfying about seeing a junior member delivering the explanation of the working tools, at the same time making it a useful proving ground for budding practitioners of the Craft.

After the Deacons have tidied away the redundant furniture and the lodge returns to its usual appearance, you will then immediately assist in closing the lodge in the third degree. If this is by virtue, then the Master may close down to the second or even down to the first in one rising, and in either case you merely repeat the Master's knocks. If, however, you close in full, then you are in action again — first with a question and answer session with the Master, and then displaying the signs with the Junior Warden. Your lodge

28

will have a traditional place where these are displayed, to some extent dictated by where items are placed on the lodge room floor, perhaps the Wardens working level with your pedestal or perhaps closer to the eastern end of the lodge. All of your words to the Senior Warden are whispered, but you go through all of the actions, and in some lodges this includes right from the first to the third degrees. In fact it is a superb opportunity for the candidate of the evening to see the correct signs from a spectator's viewpoint, so that he can change any possibly inaccurate impression he had gained during the ceremony while it is fresh in his mind, so it is almost a shame if your lodge closes by virtue from this degree. However, the third degree is usually the longest of the three ceremonies, and the brethren and caterers may all be champing at the bit to be starting the meal, so on occasions the shortened closing may be necessary.

You then salute the Senior Warden and return to your pedestal. After the Senior Warden has interacted with the Master and returned to his place in the lodge, and the Master has requested him to close the lodge, your only remaining role is a few words and the correct knocks for the Inner Guard to repeat to the Tyler.

Installation

When the year has gone round full circle, the installation will be your last meeting as Junior Warden if you are progressing towards the Master's chair. You will need only to open the lodge at most to the second degree, because if you are yet to go through the Master's chair you will have to be replaced for the inner workings of the new Master's installation, and this is usually done in the first or second degree before the Master Elect is presented for the first time. When the Past Master comes to replace you, you will already have removed your gauntlets if you wear them, and you take him by the right hand and walk him on to the platform of the pedestal from the East as you exit to the West of your chair, and you may formally present him with the gavel. You then become an ordinary lodge member until you are invited to leave before the inner workings take place.

Prior to this, after opening and perhaps also after the minutes have been read, the representative of the Provincial Grand Master will have to enter the lodge. Although you technically supervise all visitors coming into the lodge, the onus for this visitor falls squarely on the shoulders of your Director of Ceremonies or, if the visitor is of senior Provincial rank, on the shoulders of the Provincial equivalent who has accompanied him.

The only other item to be performed, that will involve you before the inner workings, is handing in your collar of office along with the other Officers. This may be done as you exit the lodge room, so the Tyler or Inner Guard can collect them all, or in many lodges the Master will personally thank those who have supported him during his year of office, and you will hand your collar to him or the Director of Ceremonies to place on a hanger in the lodge room. If the collars can be collected in a logical sequence, then their subsequent distribution to the new Officers being appointed is very much easier. Usually the juniors will hand in their collars first, effectively working backwards up the list of lodge Officers, so you and the Senior Warden will be the last ones to do so.

Whilst waiting for the inner workings to be completed, as the ex-Junior Warden you can ensure that all those not still in the lodge room are properly catered for. Your lodge may provide some refreshments for the juniors, and perhaps for the seniors as well if they call off the lodge, and you and your ex-Stewards can serve up the food and drink for the others. You might also be able to ensure that any last-minute dining arrangements, such as table plans and place cards, are properly displayed, and perhaps that the white wine is being chilled and the red wine is opened to breathe. You should also be aware that there is a recognised protocol for seating senior brethren who are attending the meal, such as the Provincial Grand Master's representative sitting at the right hand of the Master, and Grand Officers being seated further to his right. At the back of this book is one such seating plan that may be useful as a reference, although the planning for the meal beforehand should have covered that detail. All of this should ensure that the period of time outside the lodge room flies by, and you are being called back in almost before you realise it.

For Junior Wardens who are Past Masters, they may be invited to continue in office for the inner workings, or they too may be replaced. Whoever is in the Wardens' chairs will know from previous experience what is required of an Installing Warden, and almost all of the ritual in the inner workings rests with the Installing Master. You might recall during the closed session of the installation that the Installing Master's knocks may not require answering knocks from the Wardens as frequently as in open lodge, but you should be aware of the traditions of your lodge from previous installations or attendance at the practices.

As a new Junior Warden, you will have been invested by the Master and addressed by him or another brother, and then escorted to your place in the South. The Installing Junior Warden will offer you his hand and guide you into the space between your chair and the pedestal, and will then be conducted back to his seat in the lodge after you have given a court bow to your escort. You should then put on the gauntlets if your lodge has them, and watch the remaining appointments to the end of the installation ceremony. You will have a specific address delivered to you and the Senior Warden, when it is usual for you both to stand while receiving it and then to resume your seats. You then have to conduct the remainder of the lodge business and assist the new Master in closing the lodge, but all of this has been covered in a previous section and need not be repeated here.

Other Lodge Business
During the year there might be several other items of business that will occur. There may be balloting for initiates or joining members, but the onus usually falls on the Deacons to distribute and collect the ballot balls. There may be a requirement for the Wardens to announce the result of the ballot from the West and South after the Master has made his first report, and your lodge will have a form of words which they will expect you to repeat. In some lodges there is a short ceremony formally to welcome joining members which also involves the Wardens, but again you will have seen the protocol and will already know the form of words to be used.

There may be propositions, besides the possible confirmation of the minutes, when the Wardens are expected to propose and second a course of action, perhaps the appointment of auditors, etc. Most of any such propositions will occur at the business meeting where the Master and Treasurer for the ensuing year are elected, although the auditors may require a different date of appointment depending on when your financial year ends. The Wardens may also be expected to propose and second the acceptance of the Treasurer's accounts, but if you work as a pair, then because you speak last, your remarks are merely to second your brother Senior Warden's proposition.

One item that might occur during the year is that the lodge is called off. This may arise if the subject of a lecture cannot be discussed in open lodge or there may be a minor emergency that has to be dealt with and which stops the lodge business, and there is a colloquy between you and Master to do so. You will announce that the brethren can go to refreshment, and you then knock once and are answered by the Senior Warden and then the Master, but not the Inner Guard and Tyler. You then stand your column of office upright, the Senior Warden lowers his, the Immediate Past Master attends to the book, and the Deacons attend to the tracing boards. It is an unusual occurrence for the Junior Warden to initiate the knocks, and you do so again when you call the lodge back to labour, so enjoy the moment. And it is worthwhile learning the very short sentences you have to say, because it may be an unprogrammed interruption that necessitates the calling off, and it looks unseemly for a Principal Officer of the lodge to require prompting, as some have discovered to their consternation during their year in office.

The Festive Board
Unlike some other Officers in the lodge, the Junior Warden cannot relax at the festive board or meal following the lodge meeting. The Master and Director of Ceremonies will be quite prominent in the running order of the meal, toasts and speeches; the Stewards will be serving the drinks and possibly the food as well; and the Treasurer will be keeping an eye on expenditure as well as possibly paying the caterers for the meal on the same night. Traditionally as ostensible Stewards the early Junior Wardens would have been organising the last two aspects, so your duties nowadays are usefully less onerous than in bygone times, although some still remain. You will need to keep an ear open for answering the Master's or Director of Ceremonies' knocks when he calls for quiet, and the lodge may delegate you to propose some of the preliminary toasts during the evening, perhaps to the Provincial Officers.

The other main aspect of your duties is likely to be proposing the toast to the visitors, unless this is assigned to other members of the lodge on a rota. If it is your duty — and in a way it is a slightly cruel baptism of fire to have to make your first speech at the installation when you have only just been invested — there are a few guidelines worth following. Ensure your lodge traditions are followed as you preface your speech by naming the Master and others — in some lodges you will name all ranks present, in others you may be expected to restrict it to the Master, Wardens and brethren only. With any speech you have to consider your audience, not only the visitors but also the lodge members. Some lodges will anticipate a little humour being included in the speech, but be aware that certain humour can cause offence; if you are not sure, leave well alone. A short and sincere speech will never go wrong, and there is a saying: 'Stand up to be seen; speak up to be heard; sit down to be appreciated', so do not overstay your welcome. After some long meetings the meal may be running late, and those brethren keen to begin their possibly long journeys home will not kindly recall the seemingly endless minutes of trivia you decided to include for only one or two people present to understand and enjoy.

In some ways your main job is to express the lodge's pleasure that the visitors came and, if they have enjoyed themselves, that they may come again in the future. Some lodges require the visitors' toast to include how many there were and where they came from; not necessarily naming everyone, but saying there was a total of X visitors from Y lodges, and possibly highlighting those who have come long distances within the Province and from outside. This courteously recognises the time and effort they have all made to join you at your meeting. You may also be required to name the brother who will be responding on behalf of the visitors, and hopefully for him this will not be his

32

first warning of what is about to happen, but the onus falls on the Director of Ceremonies to have already spoken with him.

Your speech should not dwell too much on what occurred in the meeting or outside, which can quickly border on being self-congratulatory to the lodge. The visitor responding will hopefully want to cover what he and the other visitors have seen and enjoyed, so do not tempt him to throw away his carefully prepared speech because you have managed to leave no stone unturned. If you have ever visited another lodge and found yourself replying and have been placed in this predicament, remember how you felt and try to avoid a repetition when the tables are turned. There is a lovely sentiment expressed in the address to the Wardens: carefully imitate what you find praiseworthy in others, and what in them may appear defective you should in yourself amend. So recall those toasts to the visitors that you and the others have enjoyed, avoid the ones you have not, and select a style that you feel comfortable with — we cannot all be comedians and get away with it, but hats off to those who can.

Of course, not everyone is a superb after-dinner speaker, and some lodges prefer to delegate the toast to the visitors to other members of the lodge who are capable speakers. This can be seen as a courtesy to the visitors, but in some ways it virtually eliminates the remnants of your ostensible Stewardship, and Masonry has been carefully formulated to progressively build up the confidence of a brother in all manner of aspects. Just as the amount of work in the lodge meeting gently increases as you ascend the ladder towards the Master's chair, so the toast to the visitors may be a useful vehicle for promoting confidence in public speaking for shy or retiring brethren. You may not want to propose the visitors' toast at every meeting, and it is a courtesy to defer occasionally to another member if he has a special reason to perform the duty — perhaps because a particular friend has managed to visit — but try to propose the toast at some of the meals. The following year as Senior Warden is a relatively quiet one, and then as Master you are expected to propose several toasts and to pronounce on many other occasions, and without any previous practice this can be a daunting experience, and the short but sincere toast is just as acceptable as the professionally polished item of entertainment.

The Principal Officers' chairs and pedestals in the Cambridge lodge room. The chairs and candlesticks were presented to Isaac Newton University Lodge, No 859, in 1894 by a total of seven brethren, all of whom can be established as members and indeed many as Masters of the lodge, although the presentations were not worthy of being formally recorded in the lodge minutes!

The Senior Warden

To some extent occupying this office after that of Junior Warden does not seem a major step forward. In absolute terms you will probably be required to do less than in the previous post, and it may appear to be a quiet year ahead of you — perhaps one to take the time to watch and listen to the Master in more detail, as you will be in his position in twelve months' time.

An Outline of the Duties

On the other hand, you are now the second-in-command of the lodge, and you carry out several duties directly delegated to you by the Master which never come within the compass of the Junior Warden. These include presenting all candidates to the Master, investing them with their aprons on his behalf, and closing the lodge at the end of the meeting.

Whilst the Junior Warden has one eye on the door of the lodge, because he

has to attend to members, visitors and candidates requiring admission via the Inner Guard and Tyler, you have to keep your eyes fully on the lodge business. It is to and from you that the Deacons come and go, both of them answering to you as well as to the Master, and they control almost all of the activities not under the jurisdiction of the Director of Ceremonies. In many of the business items, it is to the Senior Warden that the Master will first turn for formal propositions, as well as sometimes to the lodge Secretary, and to some extent you are the

formal spokesperson of the lodge to the Master. Quite an undertaking, and not necessarily one in which you can relax for twelve months.

At the installation ceremony when you are appointed, you are the first appointee. The Master addresses you as his Senior Warden, and invests you with your insignia rather than jewel of office. Once installed in your chair in the West, having been advised of your duties and placement in the lodge, you can watch the remainder of the appointments unfold before your eyes, and then receive the Wardens' address. And although your first major action in the lodge thereafter is to close the lodge at the Master's command, it is probably best summarised in the next section so that the formalities of a full meeting are set out in their usual running order.

A word of warning about attending the installation meetings. If you were not able to be present at the meeting when you were appointed as Junior Warden of the lodge, you must ensure that you are present at the next installation when you are appointed Senior Warden. It does not matter if you have managed to attend every lodge meeting, practice meeting and lodge committee meeting in the two years as Warden; if you have not been formally appointed and invested at one of the installation meetings you cannot yet be considered as a future Master of the lodge. Surprisingly the reverse complies with the rules — if you make the installation and no other meeting in your year as Warden, you can be considered as a potential Master Elect, but with such an attendance track record the lodge will need some persuasive reasons for your prolonged absence before it entrusts you with the responsible position of being its Master.

Opening and Closing and the General Business of the Lodge
If you have previously served as the Junior Warden of the lodge, you will be aware of the basic elements of running the lodge. To start the lodge meeting you have to arrive at your pedestal. Some lodges allow you to make your own way there just before the meeting begins, in others you formally process in with the Master. You then continue round the lodge room while first the Master and then the Junior Warden peel off into their pedestals, and then the Director of Ceremonies conducts you into your place. You then assist the Master to open the lodge, replying as required to questions about the various Officers' placements and duties, and after answering the Master's knocks you raise your column of office to show that the lodge is formally in session.

It may be your privilege to propose the formal confirmation and adoption of the minutes of the last regular lodge meeting. Some lodges insist that you must have been personally present at the meeting to do so, and if you were absent then someone who was present should make the proposition. On the other hand, you are proposing as the formal second-in-command of the lodge, so the proposition is not a personal one but comes from the position you hold; therefore previously present or not, you should be able to propose that the minutes be accepted. After all, in your absence whoever occupied your place would have been addressed as Senior Warden, and would have carried out your duties as directed by the Master, so the lodge recognises that in some cases words and actions emanate from a certain position in the lodge room rather than from a specific person.

You may next need to propose the acceptance of the Treasurer's accounts for payment, and as with the minutes your lodge will have a well-rehearsed form of words to cover the requirement. The first practice meeting after the installation is not one to miss — you are viewing the lodge from yet another new perspective, and you may not have taken much notice of other people's words at various times during the meeting, especially those not written into the book of ritual. You will sometimes find that it is the little details in the less formalised items of business that cause you to rack your brains as to the proper words to be used, so be warned.

The lodge then moves on to the main item of business, perhaps a ceremony or a lecture. If the former you will be involved in the ritual, if the latter it may be the protocol in your lodge that it is the Senior Warden who formally thanks the speaker for his paper. This has two useful benefits: firstly you have to stay awake during the lecture and perhaps try to understand the content, and then you have to select one or two items that you found interesting to comment on in your congratulatory speech. On the plus side, there will normally be no traditional format to cover this aspect of your work, so you have a reasonably free rein as to how you approach it.

If the ceremony is other than a First, you will need to assist the Master to open up into the higher degree. For the second degree you merely remind the Master to call the brethren to order in the first degree, because the remaining interchange is entirely between the Junior Warden and the Master — you merely answer the Master's opening knocks. For the third degree you have a little more involvement, in that each Warden has four questions to answer, but again you will have been exposed to these whilst occupying the Junior Warden's office, so in part they are probably already stored in some recess of your memory banks.

From each of these higher degrees the lodge can be closed by virtue. If you want an easy life, then this will suit you, because the Master states all that needs to be said and you merely answer his knocks as required. When closing in full from the third degree, however, then you have a lot to do. Firstly there is an additional question and answer session between the Master and his Wardens, and then the two Wardens are invited to demonstrate the formal signs, tokens and words of the degrees. The Junior Warden will wait for you to perhaps reach his pedestal on your way from the West, and he will then approach you with a full set of signs, perhaps including the pass grips and words if that is your lodge tradition. He will speak quietly, salute you as a Master Mason, and return to his pedestal.

You now position yourself first to invite the Master to receive the signs, tokens and words from you, and then to communicate them to him. This time you will be speaking the words aloud, but apart from that you will be copying the Junior Warden's actions fully. You will then salute the Master, and either let him return to his pedestal or you will both move back to your places together, each holding the sign of the degree whilst doing so. After the Master confirms the signs, he invites you to close the lodge on his behalf, which you will do after his knocks. Note that whether you repeat the Master's knocks or whether you give the second degree knocks — which it could be argued you should do as you have been formally requested to close the lodge from the third degree — you should adhere to the lodge's customary method. If this full closing is performed properly, it is a very useful revision exercise for the Wardens and the brethren of the lodge, and it is something that should perhaps be done at least once each year so that the Wardens have fulfilled all aspects of their duties while in office.

In comparison the formal closing of the second degree only involves one additional question and answer of you, as opposed to the Junior Warden's double ration, and at the Master's invitation you close the lodge on his behalf. Again note what knocks you are to use, depending on your lodge tradition.

You then come to the final items of business in the meeting, when you may be required to stand with the Master at the 'risings' after answering the Master's gavel. Then once the visiting brethren have tendered their greetings to the Master, you may call the members of the lodge to stand in order to bring their own greetings to their Master. You now come to the closing, and beware of your answer to the Master about your place, because the flow of words is very similar to that in the opening catechism, and several Senior Wardens (including the author!) have inadvertently started to reopen the lodge by mistake. You may also be asked if everyone is satisfied that the business has been fully covered, and your reply may need to cover the one person outside the door of the lodge, the Tyler, so learn the appropriate words as required.

The Master then delegates you to close the lodge, after he has given the first degree knocks. In some lodges both Wardens repeat the Master's knocks, in some the Senior Warden does so and then the Junior Warden gives only one, but you may be the first to give only one knock. When the Master closes down by virtue, his statement of which degree the lodge is resumed in is

38

followed by the knocks of that new degree. By a similar token your words in formally closing the lodge have a sense of finality which should perhaps be followed by a single knock to show that the state of the lodge has changed, but each lodge has its own traditions to maintain. You also need to lower your column of office to confirm that the lodge business is ended, but you may pause slightly so that the Junior Warden can raise his and thus prevent the lodge from being in a temporary interregnum.

You then extinguish the candle or electric light after the Master has dealt with his equivalent, and then wait to be picked up by the Director of Ceremonies if you are processing out of the lodge room. He may assemble the procession and then escort the Master into position, but however this is done you will normally be placed immediately behind his right shoulder, as befits his right-hand man. After processing out of the lodge room, all of the Principal Officers may stay to greet all of the visitors as they follow you out of the room, which is always a courtesy that is well received if the geography of the building permits. And unlike the Junior Warden, you can now relax, because there are no speeches to give and the toasts are read off a formal listing, so that nothing further has to be committed to memory.

The Degree Ceremonies
While the Junior Warden is the first to check on the credentials of any candidate presenting himself to go through a degree ceremony, the Senior Warden is the one who gives him a more detailed grilling as to the recent knowledge he has been given. He is also the one who formally presents the candidate to the Master before undergoing the ceremony, and who will award the candidate with his new apron after the ceremony has been completed. Again these aspects of the work serve to underline the position of the Senior Warden as the right-hand man of the Master, almost in a way training him for the following year in the Chair of King Solomon.

The workload of the Senior Warden is much the same as that of the Junior Warden in each of the basic ceremonies, except for the longer question and answer sessions with the candidate as regards the pass grips and passwords and what he has learned in the higher degree. You will be on your feet more, and probably leaving your pedestal in order to invest the new apron, but most lodges tend not to pile any more work on to you, as they might in comparison by traditionally requesting the Junior Warden to deliver the charge after initiation. In this sense the standard progression through the offices in the lodge is designed to prepare you for your next role, and the interchanges with the Master which you have to learn during this year are already being stored away in your memory banks for the coming year.

First Degree

As noted earlier in this book, you follow the Junior Warden in being introduced to the candidate on his perambulation of the lodge. You will also need to lean forward in order to make your shoulder available for the Junior Deacon and candidate to reach forward together to strike it — this is the time when you hope the Deacon holds no latent animosity to you, otherwise your shoulder may suffer! The Junior Deacon introduces the candidate to you, and then goes through a slightly complicated manoeuvre to present you with the candidate's right hand whilst he is at the North side of your pedestal facing East. This is where having introduced yourself to the candidate before the ceremony will have given him added confidence as he goes through the ceremony. Think, for a minute, what he has gone through to be formally presented. He is in the dark, has had something stuck in him, had to kneel and stand again, gone round in a sort of circle, then performed a pirouette almost on the spot, and now someone is holding his right hand in the air. A gentle squeeze on his hand for reassurance and the sound of a recognisable voice will undoubtedly help him to take stock of his situation. And it is worth repeating — he is hopefully coming among friends, perhaps some of long standing and more who are new to him, so you and the other lodge Officers taking a short time to introduce yourselves will help him to feel at ease in this rather strange environment.

Having formally presented the candidate to the Master, you hand him back to the Junior Deacon for the next questions to be asked. As many lodge rooms are to some extent rather cramped, it is worthwhile to have practised this hand-over with the Deacon beforehand. You should not drop the candidate's hand and leave him wondering what is happening, but you may whisper to him to step forward slightly to let the Deacon slide in behind him, so that they can both shuffle into position for the questions. After these the Master asks you to direct the Deacons to bring the candidate to him. Quite why there is this apparently redundant delegation, when you only repeat what the Master has just said, is not immediately obvious, unless there is an underlying consistency with the second and third degree ceremonies when there are no additional questions after your presentation. Anyway you do as requested and the candidate is taken to the East to be obligated, and then the information restricted to the first degree is entrusted to him.

When the candidate returns to you, after a quick demonstration of his knowledge to the Junior Warden, you then give him a more searching series of questions regarding his new information. Again like the Junior Warden, you can assist the Junior Deacon by looking at him at the end of each question, having made eye contact with the candidate for most of the question — just a gentle reminder to the latter that the answers are to be dictated rather than volunteered. You should also let the Junior Deacon adjust the candidate's grip on your hand before you complete your grip on his, only correcting the candidate's grip if it perhaps slips. After these questions the Deacon and candidate perform another pirouette so that you can easily grasp the candidate's right hand for your second presentation of him to the Master. On this occasion you are delegated to invest him with his apron.

The traditional lambskin aprons for the Apprentice and Craftsman are tied in place rather than buckled. With some loose-fitting gloves, this is a guaranteed way of tying one of the ends of your glove's fingers into the knot, thereby leaving your glove behind when you have finished. I have never attempted this operation with gloves on, and it has made for an efficient way of investing him, but if you are confident wearing the gloves then by all means keep them on. In any case the Deacons can be of great assistance if the candidate is somewhat wide, when your arms may not be able to reach around his middle in order to cross over the ties behind his back, so here is another benefit of practising certain actions with colleagues before the real ceremony.

Your address to the candidate may be the short version in the standard ritual, but if you feel like accepting a challenge, why not try the longer alternative in the back of the book? For many Masons, including any recently initiated Masons who might be in the lodge that night and who have not heard this other version, it will add to their knowledge of what the apron represents, and they do say that variety is the spice of life. As always, though, ensure your lodge and in particular your Director of Ceremonies knows what you are doing — if it goes well unannounced they may not mind, but if you stumble over the new piece of ritual then there may be no-one able to help you through with a suitable prompt. Whichever version you use, there is a point when the other brethren present join in at a certain word, so make sure that you are speaking audibly for everyone to be able to hear in the lodge room. After this you can give the candidate a smile, salute the Master, and sink gratefully back into your chair, because for you the ceremony is now complete.

Second Degree

As in all of the degree ceremonies, your involvement comes some time into the proceedings. You have all listened to the preliminary questions and answers and the entrusting, and the Junior Warden has admitted the candidate back into the lodge room, questioned him on his first perambulation and let him past on his second. You then ascertain that, as the Inner Guard has stated, the candidate is in possession of the password. The candidate is then wheeled around for you to present him to the Master, after which you direct the Senior Deacon to take him to the East. Before you do so, it is usual to allow the

Deacon to reassume control of the candidate and stand ready for your directive, so hand him over and sit down, and speak only after the Deacon and candidate have shuffled into position — it all looks more composed that way.

Again you can view the obligating and entrusting of the second degree information from a distance, and after the Junior Warden's quick check on the candidate, you test him more fully. The sign is split into three separate actions, and you quiz him on all three, as well as the step, grip and word. The questions should again be started by asking the candidate and ended by looking at the Deacon so that his prompting is made easier, and then you present the candidate to the Master in order to upgrade his apron. Having tied this off with a very short address, the Master requests the Deacon to escort the candidate to the South East, and then possibly back to your pedestal for the explanation of the working tools. If it is traditional for the Senior Warden to present these, you might once more look into the back of the ritual book for the extended version of this — it is one of the most memorable pieces of ritual and well worth the effort of learning. As before, ensure that you have a local prompter if you embark on this alternative, but the extended explanation is always received with acclaim.

After the candidate has exited the lodge room and returned he is likely to be given the explanation of the second degree tracing board, which may include the extra middle section, and then there is a further piece of ritual if you are up for it — the charge after passing. Many lodges do not bother with this, possibly because it is also at the back of the book, but if you are really keen to flex your Masonic muscles you might suggest this addition to the Director of Ceremonies as well — who said this was going to be an easy year? You may, if your lodge is short of candidates and juniors, end up on a rota going back through the progressive offices, but if you are in a lodge with many juniors all of whom intend to progress on to be Master, this may be your only opportunity to hold office in the West for some considerable time. The second degree ceremony is the shortest of the three and all of these longer alternatives will fit in comfortably, so enjoy your year as fully as you wish to do and you are allowed to; some lodges guard their traditions with great care.

You then assist the Master to close the lodge by virtue or in full, the latter being only a little longer in format and with only one question for you to answer, and the business of the lodge continues.

Third Degree

Your duties in the third degree almost parallel those of the Junior Warden, but it is worth a quick résumé of what you are required to do. As in the second degree, the business starts with a question and answer session between the

Master and candidate, after which the Master entrusts him with the pass grip and password, and the candidate leaves the room while the lodge is opened into the higher degree. There are more questions to you and the Junior Warden from the Master, after which he opens the lodge. There is an additional sign for the Master to remember before the brethren sit down. As he is usually looking straight down the lodge at you, you can assist his memory perhaps by gesturing with your hands at your sides to remind him that he needs to lead the brethren in performing the sign.

When the candidate returns, as it is third degree, there will be three perambulations for him to perform. Your job is to question him on his second circuit about the second degree, and on his third circuit about the pass grip and password, and then to present him to the Master. Thereafter, as in the passing ceremony, you direct the Deacon to instruct the candidate how to move eastwards, and you can then leave the next part of the ceremony to them and the Master until you need to leave your place and also make your way to the East.

Many lodges prefer the Wardens to move as a pair rather than making their way independently to the East, so you will need to have agreed with the Junior Warden where he will wait for you, and whether you should pause so you can start walking together, or whether he will fall into step when you pass his pedestal. The two of you then displace the Deacons to flank the candidate, and wait for the enactment of the violence being described by the Master. After the Junior Warden has performed aggressively, you can whisper into the candidate's ear what is required of him, and when he has recovered you can continue with your own act of aggression. After the Master has joined in the violence, you and the Junior Warden assist the candidate to his new place in the lodge, again perhaps warning him in a whisper what is required of him.

In a few lodges there may be some perambulations by the Principal Officers, which enable you to return the large implement to your pedestal if you have not been utilising the jewel on your collar, and then the Junior Warden and you try to lift the candidate singly. The candidate will know what to expect after the Junior Warden's actions, which makes your life easier, and you report accordingly to the Master holding either the second or third degree sign as is the normal custom in your lodge. The three of you then act together, with the candidate assisting, and you ensure that the candidate is standing properly with the Master, who cannot be expected to check behind himself. You and the Junior Warden then leave the East at the invitation of the Master, and the candidate ultimately exits for a second time.

On his return you re-present him to the Master, who asks you to invest him with his own Master Mason's apron. If you have been wise, you will have ensured that it fits him correctly, as it makes for a more efficient investiture if the strap has been adjusted beforehand, so it is worth checking with the Director of Ceremonies and/or the candidate that this has been done. The traditional history then unfolds, followed by the working tools at the Master's pedestal, and the candidate sinks into his seat for a well-earned but short rest.

You on the other hand are back on your feet to close the lodge, by virtue or in full. If the latter you will first have your interaction with the Junior Warden where he whispers the key words to you, and after he has returned to the South you invite the Master to receive your communication. You then go through exactly the same sequence as the Junior Warden did with you, except you have been asked to speak up when doing so. You then salute the Master and return to your pedestal, and he requests you to close the lodge to the second degree. Note that when closing by virtue some lodges will close directly from the third to the first degree, and in others they insist on one degree at a time. The ceremony is then over.

Installation

It is at the installation that the Master Elect makes the final move into the Chair of King Solomon. In many lodges it is traditional, if the lodge has progressive offices, that the Senior Warden becomes the Master Elect. However, the installation is very much the domain of the Installing Master, who is frequently the previous incumbent, and the details of the installation for the Master Elect and Master are covered in the next sections. For now we will only deal with the formalities required of the office of Senior Warden in conducting the business of the lodge around the installation ceremony.

The lodge will be opened as normal, with the standard business of confirming the minutes and dealing with other matters such as the monthly accounts. As with the Junior Warden, if there are to be Installing Wardens invited to take over for the inner workings, you will at most need to open the lodge into the second degree so that the Master Elect, perhaps you, can be presented to the Installing Master for the first time. If you are a Past Master, you may be invited to stay in office, although in some lodges it is traditional for Masters or Past Masters of other local lodges — perhaps daughter or mother lodges — to occupy the Wardens' positions for the inner workings.

The lodge will need to welcome the Provincial Grand Master's representative, and the tradition in some Provinces is for him to enter as soon as the lodge is opened in the first degree, and in others for him to enter when the lodge has moved into the third degree. Like the Junior Warden, you will need to hand in your office collar, and leave the gauntlets on the pedestal when vacating your chair for your successor eventually to put on when arriving at the pedestal. These should not be worn by the Installing Senior Warden, as technically the lodge is in an interregnum and the gauntlets should only be worn with the collar of office by those who have been formally appointed and invested as such, but the brethren concerned should always comply with the custom and practice of the lodge.

If your lodge follows the Emulation style of ritual and inner workings, then there is very little for an Installing Senior Warden to do. You will follow the guidance of the Installing Master and faithfully answer his knocks as required, although some lodges do not expect the Installing Wardens to answer all of his knocks as the lodge is in closed session and the Tyler — possibly a junior — should not necessarily be aware of the business being conducted inside the lodge. After the installation of the new Master the Installing Master will close the Board of Installed Masters, and the lodge reverts to normal working in the third degree. The lodge may close down from the third to the second and then the first by virtue, which only requires answering knocks to those of the Master but, even if the closings are in full, you as a Past Master will be aware of the correct method of doing so.

When you have been appointed as the new Senior Warden, you will be conducted to the West, be guided into your new place by the Installing Senior Warden, and sit yourself down. If the lodge has gauntlets for the Principal Officers you should put these on, and you will have the address to the Wardens to attend, just as in all probability you did at the previous installation when you then became Junior Warden. The rest of the meeting follows the standard format until the closing, and all this has been covered before. Just be aware, as this is possibly your first appointment to the office of Warden, of the protocol of closing, especially if there is a set form of words that your lodge expects to hear. If you have been at the lodge practices and understudying the next office that you will occupy, you may have been practising the format of opening and closing from the West, so be aware that the wording for the two events is quite similar and do not start to re-open the lodge again by mistake! As this is all new to you, and there is the added tension of performing in front of usually a bumper attendance in the lodge, it is easy to transpose unthinkingly into the wrong procedure, so beware.

Other Lodge Business and the Festive Board
For many items of business the Master is assisted by his Wardens, and most of the procedures have already been covered under the Junior Warden. These

include balloting and announcing the results, confirming the minutes, propositions, and calling off and on — the last two items being easy for you as the Junior Warden says all that has to be said and you merely answer his knocks.

There is one item that is unique to the Senior Warden if your lodge has progressive offices. When the ballot at the business meeting is announced in your favour as Master Elect, you are probably expected to say a few words in response. These do not have to be many, but it is worth thinking through what you want to say in lodge. After all, you will have been forewarned — possibly at a Past Masters' meeting — there is agreement that you are the one to progress, so you cannot plead ignorance of what will happen. Of course at the subsequent festive board your health may be proposed and honoured by the brethren, and you may be requested to say something else. Both speeches can be short and to the point and, if you do have two to make, then don't let one be a verbatim repetition of the other. You will doubtless be aware that most brethren are unimpressed by long speeches that do not have much in the way of any valuable content, so short speeches will be highly acceptable to all.

Principal Officers' Chairs of Cestrian Lodge, No 425, in Chester.
The four chairs for the Principal Officers and the Immediate Past Master were
presented to the lodge on 29 May 1755 by Thomas Farrington, who was
initiated on that night. They were reputedly old even then and Edward Orme,
Deputy Provincial Grand Master, undertook to paint and ornament them. The
Master's (above) and Junior Warden's (far left) chairs are a matched pair, but
the Senior Warden's (left) has a half-upholstered back, while the IPM's chair
(see later) is of a smaller size, again with a wooden back.

The Master Elect

Once you have accepted the position of Master Elect, there are many arrangements that you will need to make quite quickly, and these will include inviting the different people to be your Officers. In many instances most will continue in office for you — Secretaries and Treasurers are usually offices that have few volunteers fighting over the right to be appointed or elected, but other offices may be regarded as progressing towards the Chair of King Solomon. Take advice from experienced Past Masters if you are thinking of advancing someone through the offices more rapidly than the norm — if a gap opens up in the line of progression to the Chair, then an opportunity has presented itself to incorporate some flexibility, but allowing overtaking in progression may seriously upset those left behind, as well as their proposers and seconders.

A different problem arises if someone on the ladder has not been able to attend lodge meetings or practices as frequently as expected. The matter should be raised with some delicacy, and again take advice from experienced lodge members if required, but during your year as Master the lodge is under your direction, and the quality of the ritual in the meetings is down to you. If because of work or domestic reasons someone cannot attend as much as he himself would wish, there is usually a harmonious resolution by the brother taking a sabbatical or even stepping aside for a while until the problem is resolved. In these circumstances he will already be aware that he is not performing as well as he might otherwise, and he will readily agree to this course of action. But also avoid the trap of wanting to choose the best team of Officers for ceremonial work that the lodge can muster regardless of the line of progression; the brother who has limitations as to his capability with the ritual but who honestly tries his best is still worthy of his place on the ladder, and you should see how you might be able to arrange support for his efforts during your year working together — both he and the lodge will appreciate it.

It may be your personal duty to formally invite all of your Officers to accept their appointments, or it may be the role of the Secretary to do so on your

48

behalf — the first sign that the lodge is there to support you in your year. The Secretary will certainly need to know the full listing, as often the banquet menu will include the Officers for the coming year, so the two of you need to interact soon after your election. If in fact the installation follows only one month after your election, that does not leave you or the lodge very much time to start from scratch. Many lodges circumvent this problem by organising a Past Masters' meeting some time before the election and business meeting, in order to discuss matters with the clearly accepted candidate for the next Master. With this consensus it does no harm for you to sound people out well in advance whether or not they are willing to take on the various offices, even if the formal letter of confirmation should strictly come from you only once you have become the Master Elect.

A problem that has arisen from time to time in several lodges is that one of the two people designated to be the Wardens in your year as Master has to step aside. The Principal Officers are usually the minimum line of definite progression to the Master's chair, and it may be that some or all of the juniors do not wish to miss out on any of the progressive offices. This may be a time to invite a member who has joined your lodge, whether he has previously been Master of his own lodge or not, if he would like to fill the immediate vacancy in the Wardens, with the understanding that he will move on to become Master of your lodge. Many joining members will be willing to volunteer to do so, happy to assist their new lodge wherever they can, and the problem will be amicably resolved. Otherwise you will be asking a Past Master of your own lodge to occupy the principal chairs once more, and again many will be pleased to do so. Be aware, though, that if no-one wants to be Senior Warden with a view to following you into the Master's chair, then you may be looking at a double year in office — the installation ceremony makes it quite clear that you can only step down from your Mastership when your successor is installed.

All of the above presumes that you as Master Elect have some say in the appointments. Some lodges prefer that the Past Masters select the new Officers and will tell the new Master who is in his team. This undoubtedly ensures that there is no untoward favouritism to be seen in any of your appointments, and it also serves to remind the new Master that he is only the titular head of the lodge, in the same way that the monarch of England is the figurehead of the country while his or her Government makes all of the key decisions for its inhabitants. It may be a courtesy that the list of new Officers is given to the Master Elect as a suggestion for him to comment on, safe in the knowledge that it will need a powerful argument to make significant alterations. And a relatively inexperienced Master Elect will probably welcome such suggestions, especially if senior Officers like the Treasurer,

Secretary or Director of Ceremonies are standing down, because the Past Masters will have a better idea of who can and is willing to take on those jobs.

It may also be your prerogative to select the banquet menu, and again the Secretary and the caterers need to know as soon as possible and the price agreed, so that potential attendees can be warned of the cost. Remember that the cost has to cover any dignitaries that it is traditional for the lodge to pay for, and these may include the representative of the Provincial Grand Master, Provincial Director of Ceremonies, Provincial Deacons, eminent lodge members of honorary status, and perhaps visiting Masters. Either the cost for the other expected attendees covers these extras, or the lodge agrees to subsidise the meal accordingly.

You will also have to decide on whom you will be inviting as your personal guests and where they will be dining, and the whole seating arrangement may be offered to you for your approval. Take notice that there may be strict Provincial protocol about the seating plan for the top table in particular, so that you are unlikely to be able to be surrounded by your cronies — plenty of time for that in the bar afterwards. And of course you will be thinking about your various speeches during your installation banquet, as well as running through the toast list with your Director of Ceremonies, so that you have a good idea of the order of proceedings for the evening event.

Some people purchase a Master's apron especially for their installation, and others may inherit one from a friend or family member. Occasionally a brother wants to keep his Master Mason's apron, and he can do so by having it altered appropriately, but this of course denies him the chance of passing that Master Mason's apron on to his son or other close acquaintance. The lodge will have its own Master's collar that you will inherit, and you will require no other collar for the year. A visiting Master is normally easily recognised in a lodge, because he has his Master's apron but no collar, unless of course he is already a Provincial Officer or the equivalent, in which case he should be wearing that regalia.

Having agreed to take on the office of Master, and indeed probably that of Warden before, you will have ensured that you are able to attend every lodge meeting, practice meeting, and lodge committee meeting during the coming year. If for some reason you are not able to do so, then the lodge should be clearly aware of what level of support it needs to give you in your year. If they are seriously going to elect you, then you will always be able to rely on their full co-operation, and they will assist you to enjoy your year in every way they can. You are the new leader of the lodge team, and just as in a football team the club captain may be injured from time to time and having to temporarily cheer on his team from the sidelines, so any unavoidable absences during your Mastership will be coped with by the lodge. But remember to give them the maximum notice so that they can rejig the team formation, and give plenty of warning to those who will be assuming the stand-in roles and having to revise the ritual they will have to perform.

As Senior Warden you will know in advance which ceremonies are scheduled to be worked in your year as Master — there may be second and third degree ceremonies to perform for initiates and Fellowcrafts already in the pipeline. You may also have been present at the interview of a new candidate, so you then know that all three degree ceremonies are required. However, you should organise a small meeting with at least the Secretary and the Director of Ceremonies to discuss how you will plan the year ahead. You may also include the Treasurer and perhaps your two Wardens, so that you can all agree on the business of each meeting and who is expected to do what. You will probably also want to discuss the social events in the coming year, so either include the social committee members or arrange a separate meeting with them. The mixture of experience and youth (hopefully) will give you the best feedback on what is occurring in the local group of lodges and in the Province in general, and also on what is the feeling amongst the junior members. On the experience side, is a Festival start or finish imminent? Are there any major reorganisations in the offing? Is anyone or the lodge approaching a significant anniversary? On the youthful and enthusiastic side, do we want or need more social events? Are the current arrangements for existing events satisfactory or could they benefit from an overhaul?

Whilst talking over aspects of the lodge organisation, you may also want to touch base with the Almoner and Charity Steward of the lodge. While you are Master you are the figurehead, and one of your duties may be to visit any infirm members and widows of the lodge, as well as at Christmas if it is your lodge custom to give presents to the latter at the festive season. The Almoner will hopefully have been in the job a while and have this information to hand, but if not then contact the previous Almoner in order to gain information about some of the older members and widows with whom you may not necessarily have had much contact. There may even be one or more members receiving relief from a Masonic source and, without breaching too much of the confidentiality about the individual circumstances, you can at least be briefed in general terms on any likely developments during your year.

The Charity Steward can update you on how any lodge or Festival funds are being accumulated, and whether or not any further impetus is required if the lodge has set itself a target and a time-scale to meet it. He can also provide you with fuller information on the various charities supported by the Craft, so that you can advise your members more knowledgeably if called upon. It may also be a tradition in your lodge that the Master is invited to select a charity to which some of the funds raised during your year will be sent, and who better to advise you than the brother with most of the information? Also if you have any ideas for an additional lodge or social activity during your year, he may also be able to suggest how, with a little bit of tweaking, the event may usefully raise some extra monies for the lodge charity funds.

So far you have discussed your future year with your lodge members, but you are about to join a group of people with whom you may interact frequently during the next 12 months, your fellow Masters in the region. Each area of the country has a local band of Masters who will find themselves visiting lodges and other functions together, and who will be attending each others' social events and ladies' evenings. There will already be a formal or informal diary of events taking place in the area in the coming year, and you will want to check that your own events do not clash unduly with those of other lodges. If your lodge has pre-booked the hotel for a dinner dance, then there is not much you can do about it, but if the date is not yet fixed then you have the opportunity to mesh in with your fellow Masters and their events. It is likely that your current Master will take you and perhaps your lady along with him to introduce you to the Masters he knows and, because lodges have their installations at different times during the year, some of the Masters will be relatively new to the job and others will be about to hand over. In the coming year, if your family and work commitments allow, you will probably be attending many events with your fellow Masters and their ladies as appropriate, and you may make several lasting friendships from among them. The social scene may be a very enjoyable aspect of your year in office, and one which you and your lady can enjoy together, but everyone will respect that your prime responsibility is to your lodge, so take heed of a gentle warning about taking on too much in the way of outside social activities that your time for your own lodge and its members is adversely affected.

The Master of the Lodge

From the viewpoint of many Masons, everything else in your Masonic career has been a prelude to taking the final step into the Chair of your lodge. If you have kept your wits about you, you will have realised that all of the interactions between the Junior Officers and the Wardens with the Master of the lodge have been training your memory banks for this year in office. As you have learned one side of each dialogue, usually the responses, the other parts have gently been sifting into your mind. In this sense the bulk of the formal duties of the Master has already been partly inculcated, and there should only be the obligations and very few other items that will be totally new to you.

An Outline of the Duties
Although your installation will be a special event for you as Master Elect, in the main you will be acting as a candidate in the ceremony, so the installation is covered towards the end of this section, similar to the preceding chapters. Instead we will begin with your duties in the meetings which you chair as Master from start to finish. And as a prelude to any of the following aspects of the duties of the Master, you will need to have attended practice meetings in order to understand fully the normal running order and details of the actions you will need to initiate. Very little will happen in the lodge room without your consent or requesting it to occur, and frequent pregnant pauses and urgent signals to you from the Director of Ceremonies are a sure indication that the Master is not totally *au fait* with his duties.

Opening and Closing and the General Business of the Lodge
To start the meeting you have to make your way into the Master's chair. Some lodges organise a procession, and in all probability the Director of Ceremonies guides you into your place between the other Officers in the procession, who have turned inwards. If it is the custom in your lodge for the Master to enter the lodge carrying the warrant in a pouch or wallet, then ensure that you have

it with you. In other lodges you may be accorded the honour of visiting Masters and Past Masters being included in the procession in front of you, while in others everyone is seated before the lodge opens. However you arrive there, you will hopefully welcome both members and visitors and express the hope that this will be a pleasant meeting for all to enjoy. The Masters of some lodges include the expression '…that profit and pleasure may be the result', but as I cannot recall any lodge meeting that resulted in pecuniary profit, I assume that both words refer to mental activities.

You may request the Organist to play the opening ode/hymn and then move on to the opening, or you may do this in reverse order. Either way, you begin the question and answer session with the Junior and Senior Wardens. You have previously learned all of the responses, and will have no doubt gained an idea of the questions, so you should be on home territory. You may direct all of the questions at the Wardens or you may involve all of the floor Officers, but you will end up with the Immediate Past Master defining your place in the lodge and the reason for your being there. There then follows a short prayer, which you as Master or the Chaplain will recite, and with your knocks you open the lodge. You remain standing while the formalities of displaying the tracing board and opening the book with its jewels are performed, the latter usually by the Immediate Past Master, and possibly the candles at the Principal Officers' pedestals are lit, and then you sit or else you or the Director of Ceremonies will invite everyone to sit.

This is probably the first time it hits you that virtually nothing will occur in the lodge without your direction, and a good memory for the conventional running order and the agenda on the summons will stand you in good stead. This is a part of the evening where the book of ritual stays silent, and each lodge will have its own routine for moving through the early business of the meeting. There will be an accepted form of words to introduce each item in turn, and again this is where an attentive ear while you have been Senior and also possibly Junior Warden will pay useful dividends, but even if you have not noticed all of the details from the other chairs, the lodge practices will help you to gain confidence about performing your duties. And it is definitely worth being confident about what you have to do; a hesitant and frequently prompted Master at the start of the meeting can affect everything that follows thereafter — it is almost like a contagious infection. An efficient and smooth delivery of even the first few phrases boosts your confidence greatly, and the lodge can seem to go almost into automatic mode, so that the lodge meeting in front of your visitors flows just as well as the best practice meetings have done without their presence.

You do not have to commit the summons to memory, and indeed you can append some notes to remind you of specific aspects of the different items as an *aide memoire*. There is nothing more irritating than forgetting to make a particular point that you have thought of mentioning at the appropriate juncture, and having to go back to cover the ground again. So use the summons as a crutch to lean on, and go through the agenda methodically. You need to confirm the minutes of the previous lodge meeting, which may require the Secretary reading them out in full, and there may be a set protocol for their acceptance to be proposed and seconded, possibly by your Wardens. You and perhaps they will need to sign the minutes as having been confirmed, and it does not matter if you did not attend the previous meeting — as Master you are signing the confirmation on behalf of the majority of brethren who have voted for their acceptance. You may next have a report from the Treasurer, and you may also take specific communications at this stage, e.g. apologies for absence which may have required other members of the lodge to fill in the necessary offices. This affords you the opportunity to thank the stand-ins for helping out, a courtesy that they will appreciate.

You will then come on to the main business of the meeting, perhaps a ceremony or a lecture. You will need to formally announce the item of business, and then adopt the procedure agreed at your practice meeting. The different degree ceremonies are dealt with in separate sections, whilst the lecture should need no further action from you, unless you are delivering it. After the completion of that item, you move on to the remaining business before the lodge. This may include a collection for charity, and you will probably invite the Deacons or Charity Steward to go round the lodge room with the collecting plate or bag. There may then be propositions or notices of motion, which you will no doubt delegate to the Secretary to organise so that he can announce the details to the brethren or introduce the members who are making the propositions, etc.

Then come the final communications of Grand Lodge, Provincial Grand Lodge, and of a general nature, for which you and perhaps also the Wardens will stand at the 'risings' in order to announce them formally. Again the ritual books are of no use in providing the exact form of words to be used, but the lodge will have its accepted phrasings which you should try to emulate. After the last set of communications the Director of Ceremonies will request visiting brethren to tender greetings from each other lodge present, and it is appreciated by the visitors if all of the lodges present are allowed to do so. They are well aware that only one or possibly two visitors will be speaking at the festive board and, without going into great lengths, each will feel that his visit has been recognised and valued by the members of your lodge. Many lodges sometimes limit the number of replies, perhaps on nights of installation, but for everyone to reply takes only perhaps 2-4 minutes and this is very little in terms of an afternoon and evening covering a meeting and meal lasting in the region of 3-6 hours, and it is a courtesy that is always well received. Every visitor is an ambassador of his own lodge, and if possible one spokesman of each lodge should be allowed to bring his personal greetings — and those of his lodge and its Master if so deputed — to the lodge he is visiting. As a Master you may well visit many lodges during your year in the Chair, and you will always want to bring your personal greetings to a new Master at his installation for example, so why not the other way around?

And finally you will begin the closing of lodge which culminates in your request to the Senior Warden to close it on your behalf. Unlike at the opening, when you had discharged the sign, you are now still standing to order. It is necessary therefore to use your left hand to manipulate the gavel — you should not drop the sign with your right hand and then recover it. After everything has been covered up as it should be, you then request the Organist to begin the closing ode/hymn, and if you are processing out of the room your Officers will begin to form the escort for you. During or at the end of the singing the Director of Ceremonies will invite you and the visiting dignitaries into the procession, including Grand Officers and maybe even acting Provincial Grand Officers to accompany you, and you will be escorted out of the lodge room. If your lodge is one of those that sing the National Anthem as well as a closing ode, you might consider singing the anthem first while everyone is still in his place in the lodge. This allows the Director of Ceremonies to form up the retiring procession during the ode; the reverse sequence of singing normally means that the procession is formed after all of the singing is completed, which just takes more time.

Remember to take the warrant of the lodge if you are expected to carry it out of the room, even if you immediately hand it over to the Secretary or Tyler for safe keeping, as you are maintaining a tradition of the oldest lodges where the Master retained the warrant while he was in office. It is a courteous personal touch if you remain at the door of the lodge room to shake hands with those who follow you out, and it is a way of you personally welcoming again the visitors and guests to the lodge, and you may request your Wardens to join you in so doing. If the evening has gone well there will be many nice things said, and even if it did not go as well as expected there will still be cheery personal comments to you as Master.

When you are opening into higher degrees there will be the standard dialogues with your Wardens, where again sufficient rehearsal and the fact you have already done it as a Warden will ensure everything goes smoothly. The only item possibly to catch out the unwary Master is the additional sign after the lodge has been opened in the third degree, and is something that is unique for the Master to introduce. For the closings there is a choice for the lodge: close in full or by virtue. The former you will have already performed whilst occupying the Wardens' chairs, but the latter is again unique to the Master: you say all of the words and your Wardens will merely answer your knocks. In some lodges the Master repeats the knocks of the higher degree followed by the lower one, in others he only uses the lower degree knocks, and there are lodges which permit closing by virtue directly from the third to the first degree and others that don't — be aware of your lodge traditions.

First Degree

If your lodge has candidates for Freemasonry, then it will be your privilege to lead the lodge team in their initiations. The lodge will expect you to perform a certain amount of the ceremony, perhaps even the whole of it, but there is an increasing trend these days for the work to be shared out among several lodge members. Not only is this a useful way of continually involving many brethren in the lodge ceremonial instead of them just watching from the sidelines, but it also means that the formal lodge work for a new Master is not too daunting. It is far better that you do what you can comfortably and well, rather than take on too much and make it an onerous job for yourself and possibly less than enjoyable for the candidate. Hopefully you will have several supportive brethren, especially Past Masters, who have delivered much of the ritual before, and so to ask them to revise part of what they have previously learned should not be too much of a chore for them. And don't forget to involve the juniors as well; if you have a large number of them, they may have to kick their heels for quite some time before starting on the ladder towards the Master's chair, and keeping them involved means they will be less likely to become disenchanted with Masonry and resign.

Probably at the least you should conduct the first part of the ceremony, up to and including the obligation, and then you may delegate the rest to volunteers. You may even be approached by the candidate's proposer and seconder that they be allowed to take part in the ceremony, and they may even want to deliver the obligation to him — the choice is yours as Master as to how much you let others do. If it is your first time in the Chair, then enjoy your year and do enough to feel satisfied that you have led the lodge for your year, but if it is your second or third time, then feel free to delegate as much as you like. But even if you elect to do very little in the ceremony, your first job as Master of the lodge on the night is to introduce yourself to the candidate. You may have sat in on the interview that he went through before being balloted for, but this is possibly a nervous time for him — definitely stepping into the unknown — and you and your members should do everything you can to make him feel at ease. You may decide to introduce him to the Junior Deacon who will be conducting him around the room, and also to the other brethren such as the Principal Officers and Tyler with whom he will be interacting. This means that both you and he need to be at the meeting place in good time, because you may have several other aspects of the evening to discuss with the members before the meeting commences.

In the meeting the Secretary and Treasurer can confirm the candidate's details and that he has paid the appropriate dues after your announcement that the initiation is the next item of business. It is usual for the obligation to be delivered from the Master's chair, and if you are vacating it in favour of the candidate's proposer or seconder you will need to be found a seat nearby. Sometimes you will displace the Immediate Past Master southwards, who in turn will displace the Chaplain, and they will need to have a vacant chair to their left into which the shuffling of bodies can take place. If, however, you want the Immediate Past Master to prompt the new incumbent of the Chair of King Solomon, then only you and the Chaplain need to move south. After the obligation, or as far as the new incumbent is taking the ceremony, you can then regain your rightful place in the lodge without too much difficulty, with the others appropriately shuffling back northwards.

If you are performing the first part of the ceremony, you have a short interaction with the Inner Guard and/or Junior Warden, and then the Deacons collect the candidate from the door of the lodge room. After the short questions and prayer, you then announce that he will be escorted around the lodge. You should speak clearly and slightly slowly because, in a full lodge room with a modicum of fidgeting, it is surprising how rapidly the human voice can be absorbed, and the candidate especially should be able to hear everything that is going on around him. It can also do wonders for settling your own nerves, and a ceremony begun well can often maintain that high standard thereafter.

You are not the first Principal Officer to receive a few telling blows from the Junior Deacon and candidate, as they merely walk past you in order to attack the Junior Warden. You then see the same enactment with the Senior Warden before he presents the candidate to you for the first time. You ask the necessary questions, taking due care in the phrasing so that it makes some sense to the candidate — even if his replies are prompted by the Deacon — and then request him to come to the East. The Deacons will bring him to you, and then just allow a moment if they are shuffling into the required position after the steps. You have one more statement and question to deliver, and then you arrange with the Deacons that the candidate is properly positioned for the obligation. Take care with the compasses, and ensure that the candidate is holding them comfortably and safely. You call the brethren to order with the gavel, perhaps more gently than normal so as not to startle the candidate

58

suddenly (the Wardens can still gavel firmly at a discreet distance), and begin the obligation.

You will doubtless have recited this several times in practice meetings before, and you will be aware that some of the sentences in the obligation are tortuously long, so it is important that the phrasing breaks the obligation down into mentally digestible pieces. Remember your own initiation, and the difficulty you had with repeating some of the perhaps overly long phrases, so try to make it easy for the candidate by using a shorter and more intelligible phrasing. There is no need to break it down to one word at a time, but neither use a long phrase that another lodge member at the practice can rattle off without thinking but that a candidate, hearing it for the first time, might forget the beginning before hearing the end. And be prepared for the candidate mishearing what you have said and stating something that needs correcting, or not remembering the end of a phrase — your brain is racing ahead over the next few phrases, but be ready for one or two repetitions. Also remember with what sign your lodge comes to order during the obligations; some lodges use the sign of Fidelity for all three obligations, while others use the appropriate penal sign for each degree in turn.

Having completed the obligation satisfactorily, you ask the candidate to confirm his obligation, having previously removed the compasses from him. You or someone else will then have to say a few words before allowing the candidate to see again, and possibly perform a few actions to co-ordinate the brethren as they join in. When the candidate can see again, allow a few moments for his eyes to adjust to the lighting, and enquire that he is ready to continue. You then point out the Greater Lights and their meanings, and help him to his feet. In some lodges you will be expected to use the appropriate grip on his hand, even though he is not aware of its significance, and you hand him over to the Junior Deacon and you or the Director of Ceremonies invite everyone else to be seated. You then introduce the Lesser Lights to him, and you must decide whether or not to keep the same order as in the ritual book. Quite why the items and the people are given in a different order is difficult to comprehend, and it all makes a lot more sense if they are consistent with each other.

Having completed that and with the Principal Officers reseated, the first explanation of what has happened is given. If someone else is performing this, he has the time to come to the side of your pedestal to deliver it; otherwise you continue from your chair. There is nothing wrong with including some actions with the explanation, as you are emphasising the seriousness of the symbolism, and those actions will bring this home to the candidate. The signs and other items are then taught to the candidate, with the Junior Deacon prompting the appropriate responses. If you are teaching the signs, make sure that the candidate is performing them properly, for instance with the proper hand and not as a mirror image, and if necessary don't be afraid of correcting an aspect of what he tries to emulate. When you are finished he should be confident about what he has to communicate — admittedly under the watchful eye of the Junior Deacon — immediately afterwards to the Wardens.

After the Senior Warden has been satisfied with the candidate's capabilities, he re-presents him to you, and then at your request invests him with his Entered Apprentice's apron. If the Director of Ceremonies carries the apron to the West, he may well show it to you for your approval before setting off with it. There is then a delightful paragraph for you to add after the Senior Warden has sat down, which emphasises that Masons should always work in harmony. If, however, it is something you want to delegate, then you might consider a junior member delivering it, as it is not a very long passage to consign to memory and could be a useful first or second piece of formal ritual for a newcomer to take on board. Thereafter comes the North East corner, and an equally delightful passage embracing the range of brethren within Masonry and their charitable considerations. This is another piece that can be delegated and, if the proposer or seconder want to assist, then this may appeal to them, as it is something that should be delivered with especial sincerity.

After the candidate has listened to an explanation of the working tools, he comes back to your pedestal to be shown the lodge warrant and to be given a copy of the Book of Constitutions and the lodge bylaws. He then retires to recover a little, and inside the lodge the participants can breathe a sigh of relief that the ceremony so far has gone well, and most certainly you can do so because your involvement is generally over at this stage. On his return he will receive the first degree charge, which is another item that his proposer or seconder may wish to deliver, or which may default to the Junior Warden. You might even consider, if the candidate has a family member in another lodge, inviting that brother to take part in the ceremony — and the charge is the favourite item to be so offered — although he may be happy to see your lodge Officers conduct all of the business of the evening and merely remain a spectator.

The candidate might also receive an explanation of his preparation for the ceremony and be formally presented with his pair of white gloves, and possibly have the explanation of the first degree tracing board given him. This contains a large amount of information, but at this stage of the proceedings the candidate is probably suffering from an excess of new information fed to him, and this may be slightly indigestible to him at this time. On the other hand, it is something that he may enjoy the next time he sees it performed, while he is sitting down and out of the immediate spotlight, as this explanation fills in many of the blanks he will have in his knowledge as he looks around the lodge room.

There is one other item that may appeal to you as Master, even if you occupy the Chair for only a part of the proceedings. For a Mason to be present when his son is initiated is always a special moment, and especially so if you are Master at the time, and there is a father-son charge that can be given during the ceremony. It is an extra and unusual piece to learn, but it is worth the effort because no matter how many ceremonies you ultimately take part in, there will be very few which involve such a close family member.

Second Degree

In many respects the second degree ceremony parallels that of the first degree quite closely. The start is different of course, as the candidate is already in the lodge room and has to answer some test questions before being entrusted with the items for re-entry. No matter how well rehearsed the candidate is, on the night he may suffer from nerves, so you should be prepared to have one or two hiccups in the responses, especially if the Junior Deacon is having to assist with some prompting. When you are practising this part of the ceremony, ensure you do it with someone who, without being unnecessarily awkward, incorporates some pauses, etc., so that you are not lulled into a false sense of security that this is something that always flows faultlessly and with military precision.

After entrusting the candidate with what he requires and his leaving the room, you need to open the lodge in the second degree. There are not many pitfalls, but remember that you are discharging a multiple sign with words and actions to suit, and unlike the other degrees the final words do not include 'for the purposes of…'. The candidate then returns, and has one circuit to demonstrate his knowledge from the first degree to the Junior Warden before you announce that he is ready for his second perambulation. The Senior Warden then presents the candidate to you, and you request that he is directed to make his way to the East. With this achieved, and after waiting for any minor shuffling into the final positions to have been completed, you warn him that there is another obligation and you then take him through it. This is much shorter than that in the first degree, and also has a shorter subsequent explanation of two of the Greater Lights this time, but remember that you may have had to hand an item to the Junior Deacon when he is supporting the candidate during his obligation.

The ceremony continues by immediately teaching the signs, etc., of the degree. As the signs are more complicated, and the explanation is fuller, try to enunciate the six-syllable word (derived from emblem) clearly so that it sticks in the candidate's mind and he is ready for the Senior Warden later on.

Master's chair of Lodge of Harmony, No 580, Ormskirk, West Lancashire
The chair back is carved and painted as a realistic three-dimensional scene looking down King Solomon's temple. At the sides of the back are a pair of dog's heads, and the chair legs also incorporate two skulls and end in claw feet. The whites of the square pavement are inlaid mother-of-pearl. A plaque notes that the design was by WBro John Ladmore, Master of Lodge of Harmony 845 (the number of the lodge when it was warranted in 1850), and also alludes to a date 5786AL, which was the year the first Lodge of Harmony 493 was formed at Ormskirk, later erased in 1838.

You can then sit back and watch the candidate repeating to the Wardens what he has just learned from you or a colleague. The candidate is then invested with his Fellowcraft apron by the Senior Warden, and the Director of Ceremonies may show it to you on his way to the West, and also the Entered Apprentice's apron on his way back. The candidate then comes to the South East corner for an explanation of his advancement and, even if you are delegating others to perform most of the ceremony, you may wish to deliver this part yourself. After the explanation of the working tools, he then retires from the lodge and again the lodge breathes a collective sigh of relief.

After his re-entrance, the candidate will probably receive an explanation of the tracing board, and possibly also an explanation of his preparation and the second degree charge. However, these will probably be performed by other members of the lodge, so you can sit back and enjoy the proceedings with the rest of the attendees. And after all of these items, you finally close the lodge down to the first degree by virtue or in full, although the latter is not very long to go through.

Third Degree
The third degree is probably the most complex of the Craft ceremonies, and certainly involves some convoluted English in its several parts. It initially parallels the second degree ceremony, but then becomes a lot more involved when the résumé and re-enactment parts are undertaken. The ceremony has some passages that are quite specific in their content and have been written with commendable clarity, and many people also enjoy hearing and even learning the traditional history which subsumes the explanation of the third degree tracing board into its content. The ceremony involves more people on the lodge room floor than in the other degrees, and more direct interaction with the Master, but then dispenses with one set of perambulations towards the end of the first half, so in many respects there are significant differences from the earlier ceremonies.

First, however, you have another question and answer session, this time in the second degree and usually with the Senior rather than the Junior Deacon there to prompt the candidate should he require it. After entrusting the candidate with the requisite information, he exits from the lodge room, and you then open up into the third degree. There are several questions that you put to the Wardens, the equivalent of which are not seen in the opening rituals of the other two degrees, and there is no prayer to be delegated to the Chaplain of the lodge because you invite Divine aid in your remarks. After discharging the third degree sign, giving the knocks, and seeing that the lodge furniture has been adjusted for the new status of the lodge, remember the additional sign that you lead the brethren in before you sit down.

The lodge room is prepared for the coming ceremony, a duty that the Deacons will normally perform, and the lighting is adjusted as they make their way to the lodge room door. The candidate returns, and after the prayer he has two circuits of the lodge room to demonstrate his knowledge of the previous two degrees, and then a final circuit to demonstrate the information you entrusted to him earlier. It is useful to remember that, whatever degree you are in, the candidate performs that total number of perambulations of the lodge room, the last of which you have to formally announce before he starts it. The Senior Warden then presents him to you, and you request that the candidate be directed on how to make his way to the East for his obligation. When he and the Deacons are in position at the pedestal, you call the brethren to order and take him through his obligation. This is the longest of the obligations, and requires the same care in phrasing as is needed in the first degree, even though the longest individual sentence in the pocket ritual book is a mere 18 lines long compared with the 20-line sentence in the initiation in the same ritual book. After the candidate has confirmed his obligation and you have explained the position of two of the Greater Lights to him, you help him to his feet.

You or a colleague then deliver the brief résumé of what the candidate has undergone before, and again the use of correct phrasing will ensure that this is reasonably intelligible to him rather than being merely several minutes of addressing him without very much comprehension on his part. You then call the Wardens to come forward and they exchange places with the Deacons, who may remain on the lodge room floor or return to their seats. Again it is best to wait until after all of the movements have been completed before the story is continued, so that the candidate is able to concentrate on what you are saying rather than on any extraneous activities around him. The story is an interesting one in itself, but do remember to pause appropriately when the Wardens are enacting those parts of the explanation with the candidate. After you have joined in with the actions, the candidate takes a little rest.

In some lodges a passage of Scripture is traditionally inserted, which may involve some perambulations by the Master and others, and which heightens the significance of what has gone before to the candidate. This is something that you will have practised with your brethren before the ceremony, in order to gauge the speed of the perambulations fairly accurately, and it can make for a delightful sequence if performed well. The passage immediately following is also a little gem, in the context of what has gone before, and then first the Wardens and finally all three of you assist the candidate to his feet, and with proper co-ordination even the largest candidates can be coped with. You finish by enacting the signs and words with the candidate, and then invite the Wardens to return to their seats.

You now explain a little of what has happened to the candidate and its significance, and then you take him through and explain the signs. You will need to be careful how you do this, because it does not look professional to topple over in the middle of an explanation which involves quite a long time standing together. The rule is not to over-reach yourself so that you may become unbalanced, and to spread your feet sideways as well as slightly forward. There are two words to communicate, a legacy of the Antients and Moderns prior to the Union of the two Grand Lodges in 1813, and if you have visited several lodges you may have heard several different pronunciations of them — ensure you use those traditional to your lodge. The candidate retires from the lodge room, which is then restored to a more normal appearance.

In Emulation working the Master performs the ceremony and the traditional history, but many lodges make a split in the responsibilities at this juncture, while some have additional splits elsewhere in the ceremony as well. If someone else is delivering this next part, you may invite him to occupy the Chair of King Solomon, or he may perform from the side or front of the pedestal, depending on the geometry of the lodge room. The traditional history is a pleasant story, and as such it has a logical sequence which is normally helpful when memorising the content. Whoever is doing this part of the ceremony should remember that, unlike the other degrees where the candidate has been invested with his new apron before leaving the lodge room, in the third degree this occurs as soon as he returns, and the occupant of the Master's chair has a few words to add to the comments of the Senior Warden. The traditional history ends with the explanation of the working tools, and again this can usefully be delegated to a junior member to give him some experience of performing the formal ritual in the lodge room. The same may be said for the charge after raising, if your lodge includes this, but the somewhat convoluted language of this charge — although the shortest of the three — possibly necessitates the attention of a Past Master. And if you do not want to deliver it yourself, this may be something for the Immediate Past Master to get his teeth into, as he has doubtless ensured that you have completed all of the essential items as required, and it would perhaps be a good way for him to round off his evening.

Your final act is to close the lodge down to the second and then the first degree. By virtue this can be achieved in one bound or as a two-step, whichever your lodge permits, but unless there is a pressing need to disappear for the meal you might consider closing in full. The demonstration by the Wardens of the formal closing is a useful reminder to the new Master Mason of the signs, tokens and words in the three degrees, and after all the candidate has just received a brief résumé of the other aspects of the first two degrees,

The Master's chair of Trinity Lodge, No 254, in Coventry

The chair depicts several jewels from the Craft and is Jacobean, while the canopy and integral front pillars are older, being Elizabethan, and were designed to have been fixed to a wall over a Principal's seat, possibly in the Old Hospital of St John the Baptist. The hospital was erected by the Knights Templar early in the 13th century, well before the establishment of the lodge in 1755.

so this would to some extent complete the revision. You should remember to lead the brethren in the extra sign once you have regained your place behind the Master's pedestal and also that, just as in the opening, there is no formal prayer prior to closing in the third degree. The full closing from the second degree takes hardly any time in comparison, and you are then ready to complete the other business of the meeting.

Installation

You have now run your full course of twelve months in the Chair of the lodge, and you are looking forward to handing over to your successor. Even if you have not had a busy year with candidates, this is the one ceremony that has to be performed each year, either in full or in the shortened version if a Past Master is going back into the Chair. It is a special ceremony if it is conducted by the previous incumbent, but it can also be easily undertaken by one or more supporters working with the Master, or to use his formal title, Installing Master. If you have had a quiet year, the Installation will contain a lot of items that are new to you, including the formal opening of the lodge into the second and third degrees, in which case you will be working hard at the end of your tenure of office.

You will hopefully open the lodge with a bumper attendance present; partly to see the last formal duties of your year, partly to wish you well, partly to welcome the new Master, and partly because this is the major lodge event of the year. The installation should attract the presence of a Provincial dignitary as representative of the Provincial Grand Master. In some Provinces he enters the lodge formally in the first or third degree, and may or may not bring a Provincial Director of Ceremonies or a Deputy or Assistant with him, and he may be preceded by a Provincial escort. Whoever announces that he is waiting outside, listen to his words carefully; if he demands admission (Assistant Provincial Grand Master or higher), you will not only welcome him as you would all of the others, but you will need to offer him the gavel of the lodge. Breathe a thankful sigh of relief if he decides to retain it, because you are off the hook with regard to the coming ceremony, but usually he courteously accepts your kind offer only temporarily and returns the gavel to you with alacrity!

With many senior ranking visitors present, there may be several formal salutes to give, and then all eyes move back to you. If you have not already despatched the first items of business you will do so now, and you may then request your Officers to line up on the lodge room floor in order to hand in their collars — a reminder that all new lodge Officers are technically appointed by the new Master except for those who have been elected. You may express a few general words of thanks for all their efforts during the year, and accept their collars so that the Immediate Past Master or the Director of Ceremonies can place them in ascending order ready for their later investiture. You will then request certain Past Masters to occupy the Wardens' and Inner Guard's positions for the installation, and perhaps also the Tyler's post if you have an extended inner workings in your ritual.

All should now be in place for the installation, and you move the lodge into the second degree so that the Master Elect can be formally presented to you. You have a few words of introduction and then hand over to the Secretary to read out the Ancient Charges and Regulations, and afterwards request the Master Elect to take his first obligation. In many lodges the Master Elect is invited to recite his obligation, but even so you should be aware of its content because you are in the best position to offer a prompt if it is needed. You then ask Fellowcrafts and soon afterwards Master Masons to retire from the lodge so that the inner workings can commence.

The standard inner workings' ceremony is relatively short, although you have all the work to do, and even shorter if a Past Master is going back into the Chair of King Solomon. This shorter ceremony is becoming more common as in many lodges the older members are recycled through the Master's chair, but done well it is still an impressive sight. If your lodge is one that has the extended inner workings there is appreciably more work to do, but even this can be split down quite easily into three or four parts so that the work can be shared out if you wish. When installing your successor, remember to allow him to put on his gloves again, and also his gauntlets if they are part of the Master's regalia. You will also be invested with the Immediate Past Master's collar before the inner workings are ended. Once you have closed the Board of Installed Masters you can relax, because the bulk of the ceremony is over, especially if other brethren invite the juniors back into the lodge for the proclamations.

Even if you continue by proclaiming the new Master, the form of words in all three degrees is virtually identical except for noting that you are doing so from the East, West and South. You then call on the juniors to greet the new Master, and remember that your lodge may request visiting juniors to join in with their greetings as well, and lead them in doing so. It all works better if the juniors know what they are doing because they have attended the practice meetings, although many lodges prefer to remind the brethren of what is required, especially in the second degree. All three sets of working tools may be presented in full or not, depending on the lodge tradition, and if they are it is again an opportunity to give the juniors their heads. The installation is a special occasion for the lodge as well as for the new Master, with a large attendance, and the juniors almost always rise to the occasion superbly — and when they do, the lodge appears healthy and confident of its future.

After the presentation of the warrant, the Book of Constitutions and the bylaws, there is the appointment of Officers, except lodges with a Hall Stone jewel will normally present it to the new Master after the bylaws. Some lodges let the Installing Master continue until the Director of Ceremonies is formally invested, others may let the latter act *ex officio* until someone else escorts him to the Master to be formally invested. It is at this stage that you hope the Officers' collars have been collated in order of seniority, otherwise there is a rapid fumbling and jangling going on in the East when an Officer's jewel is described during his investiture and it does not match the address. The responsibility for this may partly rest with you as the new Immediate Past Master, as you may be handing the collars to the Master for him to place on the Officers' shoulders, so check each collar that you are handing over.

After the investiture of the Officers and the addresses to the Master, Wardens and brethren, your installation duties are over. You then assist the new Master if he is not sure of the detailed running order through the rest of the meeting, and retire gratefully to the bar for some welcome refreshment.

The only other duties are at the banquet, when you may have been asked to propose the toast to the new Master, and you may also reply on behalf of the Installing Officers. If you wish to wax eloquent on either of these opportunities you can do so, but previously there may have been long speeches from the dignitaries present, and no-one will mind if after all of your other work you keep your remarks relatively short — remember the adage: 'Stand up to be seen, speak up to be heard, and sit down to be appreciated'.

As the incoming Master you may have very little or a lot to do on the night of your installation. Some lodges let you sit back and enjoy the occasion, leading you through the obligations and all of the other aspects of the installation itself, and having other members of the lodge delivering the various addresses to the new Officers. Other lodges will expect you to learn only your first obligation, as the Installing Master has plenty of other work to perform, while some lodges expect their new Master to be led through the installation but then formally to invest each of his Officers personally and in full — quite an undertaking. Unless there are peculiar circumstances that propel you unexpectedly from Junior Warden to Master in one bound, at least you will have had plenty of warning. But if you are not a capable ritualist do not despair; it would be a singularly unfeeling lodge that tries to force one of its members to take on more than you can comfortably achieve, and thereby spoil what should be the highlight of your Masonic career to date.

If other lodge members deliver the addresses to the Officers, you can still personalise each of their appointments with a few words of your own. You will need to learn the short address to the Immediate Past Master whom you invest during the inner workings, and you will then receive the address to the Master. If you wish to choose someone special to deliver it, perhaps your proposer or seconder, or even a family member who may not be in your lodge, then your request will probably be readily acceded to by the members of the lodge in order to maximise your enjoyment of this special occasion.

After the completion of the ceremony of installation, reality hits you with a bump — there is still the remainder of the lodge business to complete and then the lodge to be closed, and very little will happen from now on in the lodge without your direction. A wise Director of Ceremonies will have ensured at one or more of the practices before the installation that you have gone through the motions of completing the formal business and closing the lodge, so hopefully you will be able to go to some extent on automatic pilot. For many items of business you immediately refer to other lodge Officers to do something, mainly the Secretary, so that you are able to follow the agenda as a series of prompts, and you can make notes on the summons about whom you will call on to act. No-one will mind you glancing occasionally at the

Director of Ceremonies or the Immediate Past Master to ensure that you are not leaving out any significant item. The 'risings' and the closing of the lodge you have usefully performed several times beforehand as one or both Wardens, so hopefully these aspects should be largely comprehended already.

Having left the lodge room, and probably paused outside to receive the personal congratulations of visitors and members alike, be warned about immediately quenching your thirst at the bar. In all probability drinks will be provided on the tables, and you will need to pace yourself, and there will be no shortage of friends and members wanting to buy you a celebratory drink. One important item at least you have to deliver *in compos mentis*, and that is your reply to the toast to your health. It would be a shame, having worked really hard to ensure that all of your formal duties in the lodge were performed satisfactorily, to let yourself down by being slightly inebriated for this reply. You will know your own capacity for alcohol, so take care not to exceed it — there will be plenty of time after the banquet to indulge yourself if you are so inclined, either in the bar or at home with a few or several close friends.

Other Lodge Business

There are several other items that you have to cover as Master of the lodge in its general running. You should be aware of the content of each summons, although the Secretary will organise the compilation and printing for you. There may be other items that should be included with the summons from time to time, such as announcements for social events and ladies' evenings, as well as copies of any key correspondence from Grand or Provincial Grand Lodges. You may need to agree with the Secretary and Director of Ceremonies how unusual items are dealt with efficiently in the lodge, rather than winging it on the night in the hope that the others can keep up with you. The food to be ordered for each festive board may also be under your jurisdiction, and there may be other occasions such as the Olde English Nights and Burns' Suppers that your lodge enjoys and which require a special menu.

You should also be aware of the regular practice meetings that the lodge has, probably one or two weeks before each lodge meeting, because you as the head of the lodge ought to be there. The practices are to assist all Officers in brushing up their ritual for the coming meetings, and you will need to run through the various items of normal and unusual lodge business that need to be dealt with. It is most important that you lead from the front; the brethren, seeing you put a lot of work into mastering (!) the ritual you have to perform, will be inspired to put in a similar effort to assist you, but an opposite attitude from you may lead to having a similarly opposite effect on them. And the practice nights are when the pressure is off, and you can quietly confirm what you already know and what you need to concentrate on, as you will have doubtless found when attending practice nights whilst working your way through the ranks.

If yours is a popular lodge, there may be people queuing up to join you — as existing Masons who will be joining members, or as members of the public who wish to become Masons. You may even have a family member, perhaps a son, whom you wanted to be initiated during your year in the chair, and in this case you will have probably pencilled his name into the list of people wanting to become members of the lodge. Remember that words about a lewis (or son of a Mason) taking priority over any other candidate only apply on the night of initiation itself, not to jumping the queue if there are several people already proposed for membership, so you will need to have planned for the event. And to initiate any family member or close friend, and especially a son, is a special moment for any Mason, so make sure the ground has been properly prepared.

Whatever category the new member belongs to, joining or candidate to be made a Mason, he will have to be formally proposed and seconded in open lodge at one meeting, and then balloted for at the next or subsequent lodge meeting. For this to occur the candidate for initiation will need to have been interviewed by lodge members or a lodge committee, depending on your bylaws, his application cleared by Province as necessary, and his appropriate details circulated on or with the lodge summons. You will then announce that the ballot is about to be conducted, you or the Secretary read the details with the summons, and you invite the Deacons to prepare for the ballot. You may show the brethren that the single drawer, or the 'nay' drawer if there are two drawers, is hiding no residual balls. As Master you may vote first or last, and either the Deacons will distribute the balls and collect them (both for the ballot and the left-overs), or the lodge members will make their way to the balloting station in the lodge room, and you will then announce the result of the ballot.

If the ballot has proved favourable, you will happily announce so, and your Wardens may be called on to repeat the result from the West and South. If, however, there are more negative votes than are allowed in your lodge bylaws, then the candidate is rejected for the time being, but if there are two or more candidates — and joining and initiation candidates can be balloted for together — then the ballot must be split and retaken in order to resolve where the problem lies. There may of course be no problem and one or more brethren may have made a mistake, and if there has been an adverse ballot you may ask if any member has done so, but do not expect a full response as some will be too embarrassed to openly admit their error. The reason for

71

many lodges preferring to ballot on one night and initiate at a later date is obvious, if you stop to think of the potential embarrassment to the lodge and candidate if the latter has to be told his election to membership has failed on this occasion.

Balloting for the Master Elect and Treasurer at the business meeting, and for the Tyler if he is not a member of your lodge, is performed differently. The Master Elect can be chosen from any of the members with the correct credentials: those of having served as a Warden or indeed as a Master in any lodge in the English Constitution. This includes both Junior and Senior Wardens of your lodge if they have not previously been installed as Master, all Past Masters of the lodge, and all joining members with the equivalent qualifications. A ballot using balls is therefore inappropriate, and the Secretary will have prepared ballot slips on which each member of the lodge writes his choice. As Master you introduce the ballot, and you can confirm the normal lodge tradition (if one exists) of inviting the Senior Warden to be put forward for Master Elect, and confirm that he has expressed a willingness to take on the responsibilities if elected. The Deacons distribute and then collect the ballot slips, and you — probably assisted by the Immediate Past Master or another senior lodge member — sort out and read out the votes cast. You then declare the result of the ballot, and the Master Elect usually rises to thank the brethren for the confidence in his capability as expressed by the ballot.

The ballot for Treasurer is also by ballot slips, but the credentials are more limited: who is actually willing to undertake the work? Often the Treasurer continues for several years, and if he has contained the increases in lodge subscriptions to within commendable limits, then long may he so continue until someone else volunteers. Frequently the Treasurer will be a Past Master, although suitably qualified juniors would be equally welcome, and the previous Past Masters' meeting will have discussed the options thoroughly. You again read out the names on the returned ballot slips, and the Treasurer Elect also rises to thank the brethren for their confidence placed in him. The vote for the Tyler can be by a show of hands, because if one person acts as Tyler for several lodges in one Masonic Hall, then he will be well known to all the members. If the lodge bylaws call for the election of the Tyler at the business meeting, and on this occasion he will be a lodge member, then a proposition can be made that his appointment be left in the hands of the Master Elect, and this can be seconded and agreed on a show of hands.

It may be that during your year the lodge or one of its members will celebrate a significant anniversary in a long Masonic career. Some Provinces help lodges to celebrate every 50 years of existence, for others they may

72

even enjoy the 25-year interim celebrations. For individuals the 50-year landmark is seen as important, whilst the 100-year anniversary is surely beyond anyone's capability (the best I have noted to date is over 80 years in Masonry). Most Provinces will normally send a senior representative to conduct the proceedings, and for a centenary or bi-centenary will probably send a full Provincial team, and the organisation for such an event will require significant additional planning. The lodge may need to update its history, perhaps invite its mother and daughter lodges to celebrate with it, perhaps contact those ex-members who have moved away from the area who may wish to return for this special occasion, etc. For this purpose it will be necessary to set up a small committee to share the workload, otherwise the Secretary will probably blow a gasket under the plethora of items he will have to cope with. Be warned that this may pose an additional burden on you — even one or two years ahead of the celebration — in chairing a committee to co-ordinate the compilation of a history and other aspects of the event, and try to stick to the agreed timetable in order to complete the project on time as a publication produced some weeks after the occasion loses some of its lustre.

The formal lodge meetings on these celebrations will be relatively easy to cope with, as the Provincial representative will probably conduct the proceedings once he has entered the lodge room, and you can sit back with the rest and enjoy the meeting. The banquet will probably also have a strong Provincial feel to it, and may be under the direction of the Provincial Director of Ceremonies or one of his Deputies or Assistants. And though you are in the chair of the lodge, there will almost certainly be members of greater seniority who should take centre stage on these occasions — especially if it is their personal anniversary — so have the forethought to let them have their heads, and it should be a night for everyone to remember for hopefully all of the right reasons.

But even if the Province limits its attendance to only these significant occasions, there is nothing to prevent a lodge from organising its own events — perhaps in its early years celebrating every decade, for example. You are perfectly capable of inviting your mother and daughter lodges, perhaps other lodges in the vicinity, perhaps the consecration team or whoever is left of it, and many others. It does no lodge any harm in finding one or two events to celebrate every now and then, so that there are several high spots in the lodge's history over the years. And even if without a formal Province presence, perhaps by way of a change of style, colleagues and contemporaries could review the individual's career in Masonry or the lodge history with personal anecdotes and reflections on the contributions in the lodge and to the Craft in general. All of these events are more likely to happen if you as

Master indicate that you would like to see them take place and that you are willing to contribute in any way possible, even if you are a relative newcomer to the scene, and your year will be embellished accordingly.

You may require extra lodge meetings in your year, and the Secretary will have to apply to Province for dispensations to hold them. These may be special celebrations that fall between lodge meetings or in the period when normally the lodge does not meet, during the summer recess for example, and the lodge wishes to meet on an exact date. Hopefully these meetings will be enjoyable events, and the summons which includes the business of the meeting will follow the lines of the regular lodge meetings. It may also be necessary to hold an emergency meeting, to resolve formally some issue in the lodge that you do not wish to rehearse while visitors are present (remember you can invite visitors to leave before you close the lodge at any meeting, so that the members can complete their remaining business *in camera*). At any emergency meeting the only items of business are those set down on the summons by the Secretary; there can be no discussions on any other item of business at one of these special meetings.

Lodge Committee Meetings

It is in the lodge committee meetings that much of the discussion on

different topics should take place, rather than in the lodge room, and you as Master will be required to chair the meetings. It is important that everyone feels confident that he can offer his opinion on any topic taken at the meeting, but it is equally important that you are able to limit the excesses that can occur if a totally free rein is given. The whole purpose of this meeting is that liberal discussion can occur between members that you may not want to air in the presence of your visitors at a formal lodge meeting.

An early Master's jewel from St John's Lodge, No 191, in Bury, East Lancashire.

74

Two King Solomons, one (left) from Tranquillity Lodge, No 274, in Rawtenstall, East Lancashire, and the other (right) from Cestrian Lodge, No 425, in Chester. The first is only brought out for installation meetings, while the latter is permanently on display in the lodge room and was presented to the lodge in 1866.

and that any dissension is hopefully amicably resolved before it can generate a real head of steam. If you have not chaired such meetings before, then remember how they have been handled in previous years, and also agree with the Secretary beforehand a list of agenda items that will ensure that all pertinent matters are discussed appropriately. The Secretary will also be able to remind you whether the meeting is open to all members or only to some, perhaps Past Masters, but this should be detailed in the lodge bylaws.

You will perhaps have the minutes of the last committee meeting to endorse, with any corrections as required, and the Secretary may have a draft agenda to cover most of the usual topics. These will include correspondence from Grand Lodge, Provincial Grand Lodge and from your local grouping of lodges, as well as general communications. Not all of these need to be repeated in the lodge room, which will make the formal meeting more efficient in the use of its time, but there will be some items that need to be formally recorded, and this is the time to agree them. There will be other topics such as those from your Masonic Hall that will require action, especially as such items will affect the future annual subscriptions you will have to agree on together — and the Treasurer's report will be first presented to the lodge committee. And there will be several aspects peculiar to your lodge, such as assessing future Officers of the lodge, recommendations for potential Provincial honours, possible candidates or lectures in the coming months, organising special events, and so on. As each topic is discussed and then closed, it will be useful if you can précis what the ultimate conclusion was, which will ensure that every attendee is aware of the outcome, and will greatly facilitate the job of the person taking the minutes of the meeting.

Interviewing Candidates
The interviewing of the candidates for Freemasonry will be performed by a group of members, preferably not too many so that any candidate is totally overwhelmed by the numbers, and as the Master you should try to be there. In fact, the lodge bylaws may decree that you and a certain number of other members have to be there for the meeting to be quorate. Over the last few years the style of such interviews has changed somewhat, and they are much less formal than they used to be. It is to be hoped that when the candidate attends for the interview he will be accompanied by his proposer and/or seconder, as the people who have previously known him best.

There are certain items which have to be included in the interview, and pre-eminent among these is the request that the candidate affirms he believes that there is a Supreme Being; without this confirmation there is little point in continuing the interview any further. And you should ask if there are any convictions or other offences that should be taken into consideration over his application — not that all or any of them may bar him from joining, but certain occurrences have to be pointed out to Grand Lodge for it to deliberate on.

As well as allowing the members of the lodge who are present to raise any issues that they might want to do, and you will doubtless have introduced everyone at the start of the meeting, you should also ask the candidate if he has any questions to put to the members about the Craft. There may be items of concern to him that can be readily resolved, so that he can join without any misgivings, however slight. And he should also be advised about the initial joining fee and the annual subscriptions that he will be expected to find, so that the financial requirements do not come as a surprise to him. You should finally thank him for coming to the meeting, and advise him that he will be contacted as soon as Grand Lodge has approved his application if necessary and the lodge has balloted for him to become a member, unless you are intending to ballot and initiate on the same night. After the meeting, you as Master will have the application form to countersign that the interview has taken place, even if you were not present at the meeting, so that the Secretary can formally announce before the ballot takes place that you have approved the application.

The Festive Board
After the lodge meeting there is usually a festive board, over which you preside, the menu of which you and/or a committee of lodge members may have selected. Your lodge will have a traditional layout of the room for such occasions, with the Wardens strategically placed, which is perhaps modified when there are large numbers of people present on special occasions. A possible table-plan is included in the Appendix if you are not sure of the formalities, but your lodge customs should be maintained where possible. You may begin the proceedings at the head of the table, or you may be applauded as you walk to your place; if the latter some people are upset if there is any slow hand-clapping, but take it in good humour — in this instance applause is applause. You will normally gavel for quiet while grace is said, by you or the Chaplain of the lodge, and then the meal begins with you being served first. This usefully means that you should finish the course first, and you are then ready for any wine-taking that you wish to indulge in. The Appendix includes a possible order of wine-taking and toasts, and the key message is not to over-indulge in the pastime; by all means incorporate any special occasions as appropriate, but consider taking wine with everyone in turn after the first course, and let the brethren enjoy the rest of the meal without further incessant interruptions.

If you have conducted an initiation, then the Entered Apprentice may, but not always, be seated on your immediate right. You should ensure that you devote much of your time to talking with him, as he will still be wondering what sort of organisation he has joined after going through an unusual and formal welcoming ceremony in the lodge. If you direct your mind solely to other items, however important to you, his first impression of Masonry may be adversely coloured by your lack of attention, and you should not expect the senior brother on the candidate's right to ensure he settles in well. After all, that senior brother may be a visitor and the candidate has joined your lodge, so you should look after him. He will probably be aware that he is expected to reply to his welcoming toast, but may want to check the exact form of words he needs to use when commencing his speech, so be prepared to assist him. Of course, in some lodges the candidate is seated with his proposer and seconder who will obviously shepherd him through his first festive board, and your workload is thereby diminished. It may be a thoughtful idea to have a special copy of the summons printed with a blank extra page incorporated, so that all of the attendees at the festive board can sign it as a memento for the initiate to keep, just as at many installations a menu will often be signed by all attendees for the new Master to retain.

After completing the meal you will probably gavel again to return thanks, and then propose the loyal toast. If you have sung the National Anthem at the close of the lodge meeting, there is no need to do so again, while in some lodges the anthem is not sung at all during the evening. If it is sung at the festive board, you as Master normally propose the toast, sing the anthem, and then everyone raises their glasses in response to the toast. The next toast is to the Grand Master, after which the brethren may be allowed to smoke, but smokers should check when visiting lodges as to what protocol is followed — these days some lodges are non-smoking and smokers retire from the room. If there is to be any formal singing, such as the Master's song or the Entered Apprentice's song, the singers may appreciate a smoke-free atmosphere so that their vocal chords are unaffected, and smoking may only be permitted after they have performed. As a further aside, if your lodge indulges in fire after each toast — recalling the old tradition of banging drinks' glasses on the table (preferably empty and definitely using toughened glass) as an accolade to the toast — then try to emulate your predecessors in the way you introduce and conduct the firing.

There is then a standard list of toasts which your Province will issue, so that the senior Provincial Officers are correctly named, and the Secretary or Director of Ceremonies will hand you this as required. It is useful if you can involve the Wardens in proposing some of the toasts, especially if your lodge has firing after the toasts, so that they have a little experience of such items at the festive boards before they become Master and have a great many toasts to do in that capacity. They could for example share the Grand Officers' and the Provincial Grand Officers' toasts between them, and the Junior Warden often proposes the toast to the visitors as well.

You will then have your health toasted by the Immediate Past Master or perhaps another colleague, and you have the opportunity to say a few words. The emphasis should be on the few, especially if you have led a long ceremony in the lodge previously, and even if you are a superb raconteur you should restrain yourself — the persons proposing the toasts to the candidate or visitors and their responses are preferably not to be overshadowed by your speech as Master. A little forethought is always worthwhile, even if you can usually speak in an off-the-cuff manner, because it will prevent you from forgetting something that was worth saying. You will obviously want to cover certain items, and perhaps advertise some coming lodge events, but as Shakespeare said in Hamlet: 'Brevity is the soul of wit'. At your installation the Master's song may be performed before your speech, and for many people this is a particularly moving occasion — when the warmth of the affection of lodge members and visitors is almost tangible — and you may need a few moments to collect your thoughts before commencing your reply.

After your reply there is a miscellany of toasts, with additional ones at installation banquets such as the Founders of the lodge, etc., and all of these may be relatively short. You eventually summon the Tyler to propose his toast, perhaps with a double knock, and then you normally have the final word to wish people a safe journey home. If it is the custom in your lodge to announce the charity collection, you might delegate this to the Charity Steward, as he is the person doing all of the hard work in gathering contributions by various means, or you can state the amount in your concluding remarks. You may then have a bar bill to settle if you have had some guests at the meal, and tie up any loose ends with the Secretary and Director of Ceremonies as well as confirming any arrangements for practices, etc., before the next lodge meeting. Whilst you are the titular head of the lodge, you will find these two officers invaluable assistants in helping to make your year run as smoothly as possible and, unless you are an experienced organiser, lean on their services thankfully.

If the lodge hosts a ladies' dining-in night, when they and other non-Masons may be present, then the number of toasts is usually severely curtailed. You may for example toast the Queen and the Craft, the Grand Master, obviously the ladies, and then all of the other visitors. If there are any initiates, then their health should be toasted and they should be allowed to reply, but there will be less reference to Masonic items and what took place in the lodge meeting than when only brethren are present. Although these events have much less formal Masonic protocol than the usual festive board, they are none the less very enjoyable occasions, as well as being evenings when you do not have to leave your lady alone at home for the umpteenth time that month.

Social Activities
One of the pleasantest aspects of your year in office is that you may be the formal host on behalf of the lodge for many social events. Your lodge may

have several regular activities each year, such as socials and ladies' evenings that may need to be booked several months or even more in advance, and also Olde English nights or Burns' suppers after the certain lodge meetings. You may also decide to hold new events during your year, such as a ladies' dining-in night after one of the lodge meetings, perhaps near Christmas, as a way of introducing some variety into the current list of enjoyable occasions. You can also invite any widows of previous lodge members to join you at a dining-in event, while they may be more reticent about attending a lodge social or dinner dance unaccompanied.

A word of warning; you should be careful not to promote too many new events, unless you are in a lodge which has been baying for more social occasions for some time. You will find that the organisation will fall on the shoulders of only one or two people for many events, and they can become overloaded. It is probably better to introduce only one or two departures from the norm in your year and, if the lodge enjoys these, then your successors can build on your example in future years.

If your lodge has several social activities that involve the ladies, then there is probably already a smoothly running organisation in place, and this may include a social secretary and treasurer to relieve the equivalent lodge Officers of these extraneous activities. If your lodge runs several successful events annually, then it is probably not a good idea to cause a tremendous shake-up in your year, but by all means introduce one or two minor variants on the theme. Whatever back-up team you have, they will assist you in discussing how best to implement your ideas and caution you if you are about to proceed down a route that has been tried previously but with limited success. You should also not attempt too ambitious a ladies' evening or other social occasion; remember that the ticket price should cover the costs of the event without requiring any supplement from the lodge funds, and that your successor may be in the invidious position of trying to compete with the Lord Mayor's Show.

Often at a ladies' evening there is a song sung to the Master's lady. Some lodges use an adaptation of the Master's song, while others prefer not to and select other appropriate songs for the occasion. You may be lucky to have good singers and accompanists in your lodge, or you may know of singers in other lodges who would be willing to do it for you — in fact one of the benefits of getting to know your fellow Masters is that between them they will be able to recommend people to fill in any gaps you may have in the entertainment for many occasions as well as the formal ladies' evenings. It is one of the most useful pieces of networking you can come across in your Masonic career, so make the most of their helpful advice.

The main concept is to make sure that all of the ladies enjoy themselves, especially yours after having spent the last year ensuring that you are turned out for each lodge meeting as immaculately as you let her, so ensure that she in particular enjoys her event. Each lady offers tremendous support throughout the years to her man, often with very few quibbles, and to give the ladies a formal thank you occasionally is always well appreciated. And although this section of the book has been written almost totally with the formal lodge activities in mind, bear in mind that this is a special year for both you and your family to enjoy, so embrace the opportunity as fully as you want or are able to.

Having completed all the duties of your office, hopefully to your own and your lodge's satisfaction, you will be looking forward to resting on your laurels for a while. During your year you will have tried to maintain the lodge's traditions as best you can, you may have suggested new ways in which the members can further enjoy their Masonry, and you will have become the latest statistic to be entered on to the lodge summons or display board of the list of Masters. Even if you are invited to re-occupy the Chair of King Solomon at some time in the future, the first time will always be special, and hopefully one of the most enjoyable times of your life — congratulations on a job well done!

The Immediate Past Master

An Outline of the Duties

If you have travelled through the several progressive offices on your way to the Master's chair, you have literally almost seen it all; done it all; and now have the Immediate Past Master's collar to prove it. Note that if you have to miss your installation hand-over, you cannot technically be formally invested with your collar, as this is done in the inner workings. You can turn your hand to anything, and in many lodges you will from time to time be invited to do so without much delay, but your first duty is to support the new Master in his year of office. You are therefore placed at his left hand, so that he can receive instant advice on any matter that arises in the lodge, and you should also be prepared to prompt him at any point in any ceremony.

If you are a good ritualist, there is no problem; if the new Master is a good ritualist, there is again no problem. If, however, these two criteria are not fully met your assistance, as requested when you were invested with your collar, may be required on several occasions. If you are not confident that you can give the correct prompt at every point of a ceremony, then you should consider delegating the job to a supportive Director of Ceremonies, or even using the ritual book yourself for the prompts. The alternative is that you may give the incorrect prompt, which can throw the Master into even more confusion than he is already coping with as he comes to a halt, and that is unforgivable. Although you should not make your use of the book too obvious, and in the third degree it is sometimes difficult to read during the ceremony, it is probably the lesser of two evils by a considerable margin. In other Constitutions a large part of the ceremony is read out to the candidate rather than memorised, but that is not the norm in the English Constitution and most would feel that the candidate will gain a better appreciation of what is being said when a piece of ritual is delivered competently from memory than by almost any other method.

You should keep yourself briefed with the business of each lodge meeting. The new Master, even if in perfect health, may be taken ill at short notice or have to be absent due to business or family commitments. In his enforced absence, you will in all probability be called on temporarily to re-occupy the Chair of King Solomon. The opening and closing of the lodge and the general items of business should cause you no problems — you spent the previous year doing them at every meeting — but if the Master had agreed to undertake a large part of the coming ceremony, then you should be aware of what is required of you in his stead. You will probably have understudied the Master or volunteered to be the candidate at the recent practice meetings, so you will have at least relived the ceremony in your mind, but even so there will hopefully be a telephone call to give you as much notice as possible that your services will be in demand on the night rather than only being informed at the meeting. If in your year of office you did not have the opportunity to perform a particular ceremony, then you may elect to remain as Immediate Past Master, and someone else with prior experience will stand in for the Master. The title 'Past Master' is not gained without some effort, and with your experience you should be able to cope at short notice with almost anything you have previously done, but there are limits for even the best of us!

With regard to the other aspects of running the lodge, your previous year in office can stand you in very good stead. And sometimes even a very competent new Master who is an excellent ritualist can be temporarily perplexed by items not covered in the ritual books; he realises there is a standard form of words for each item of business, but will often appreciate a quiet kick-start into the wording required. You have very little to do practically in the lodge, probably opening the book and adjusting the jewels as required, and closing the book at the end of meeting with an appropriate valedictory sentence. In some lodges it may also be the custom to delegate some parts of the ceremonies to the Immediate Past Master, and one of the favourites is the traditional history in the third degree. If you have not performed this before, it is an enjoyable story to retell, and this in itself assists in the process of committing it to memory. And if you are not one of the great ritualists in the lodge, you can always share the work between other members, perhaps the signs and working tools at the end, which can lend themselves to be delivered by some keen and capable junior members of the lodge.

Other than that, if your lodge normally shares the ceremonial work between several brethren, you may volunteer to assist in one of these roles, and if you want some additional work you may volunteer to deliver the charges after passing or raising. These are items that are rarely done in many lodges, and they are both quite complicated to enunciate, but they may serve to make a pleasant change from the standard ceremonial package. Beyond that, your year will be spent watching the competent team of Officers progressing onwards towards the chair that you have just vacated, and perhaps turning your mind to what role you can play next in the lodge. Some lodges may immediately kick you out as Tyler, which usefully gives you a role to play after your two years in the East, and it has sometimes been said that at no time do you feel more at a loose end than 'immediate past Immediate Past'. However, in many lodges you may soon be directed into the offices of Assistant Director of Ceremonies, Secretary, Chaplain, Almoner, etc., depending on where your talents may be required in the lodge. No doubt if you have enjoyed the ritual side of Masonry, you will be happy to be pressed into service in many future ceremonies, even if not being given a specific office after your retirement from the East.

Other Lodge Business

One of your pleasant duties at the festive boards is to propose the continued health of the Master. You obviously have a vested interest in this; if he enjoys good health in his year and attends every meeting, then you have an easier year by his side. And if he has been able to put in plenty of hard work to learn what he was required to do, then he has simplified your back-up role considerably, and he should be congratulated for doing so. Some lodges may enjoy a blow-by-blow and detailed account of everything that happened in the lodge, but most will prefer a few words from you as a prelude to toasting the health of the Master and then listening to what he has to say.

At the end of this year you will no longer have a reserved place at the festive board, a privilege you have enjoyed for four years as a Principal Officer and then as Immediate Past Master, but on the other hand you can now rejoin your drinking cronies elsewhere. Hopefully there will be the quiet satisfaction of several jobs well done and with your talent, as said before, most lodges will very shortly find you other work or an office within the lodge to keep you busy. And if you still feel at a loose end, there are many more side degrees to join in Masonry if you wish to flex your muscles in new directions.

(See opposite)
The Immediate Past Master's chair of Cestrian lodge, No 425, in Chester. The date of 1768 is carved into the back of the seat (possibly during the restoration of the old chair), together with the Latin expression 'Aude, Vide, Tace' — 'listen, look and be silent' — in popular use in lodge furniture and banners during the 18th and 19th centuries.

Appendix

Procession Into and Out of the Lodge Room

If your lodge has a formal method of conducting the Master and his Wardens to their respective positions in the lodge room, the incoming procession may well include:

Assistant Director of Ceremonies		Director of Ceremonies
Tyler		Inner Guard
Junior Deacon		Senior Deacon
Junior Warden		Senior Warden
	Master	
Immediate Past Master		Chaplain

It is noteworthy that the senior of two lodge Officers is on the right-hand side of any pairing, and is therefore walking closest to the centre of the square pavement, and this is a general principle adopted in most lodges. If your lodge invites visiting Masters and Provincial Grand Officers to join the procession, they will normally fit in between the Director of Ceremonies and the Deacons, and then everyone stops and turns inwards to form a guard of honour for the Master to pass through into his chair. These additional members of the procession may be in order of seniority, juniors first, and they will find their seats around the East of the lodge room after the Master has taken his place. The Immediate Past Master and Chaplain will also stay in the East, leaving the remaining lodge Officers to escort the Wardens to their positions. The Junior Deacon will step into his place once the Senior Warden has arrived at his pedestal, the Tyler and Inner Guard will peel off to the door if that is situated in the North West, and the Senior Deacon will follow the Director of Ceremonies and his Assistant to his seat in the North East and near to the Master.

The retiring procession is almost the same, except that the Assistant Director of Ceremonies stands alone at the front while the Director of Ceremonies is escorting the various brethren to their places in the procession, and the latter normally remains in the lodge room as the procession exits. The Wardens will also follow rather than precede the Master, as this time they are not forming a guard of honour as the junior Officers will do. Some lodges insist on placing every brother according to rank, while others invite selected brethren only, such as the representative at a meeting, visiting Masters (especially if a lodge is making a formal visit), and Grand Officers, but each has its own traditions. The Deacons may cross their wands for brethren to pass underneath at both the incoming and outgoing processions, whereas the Tyler and Inner Guard will find it more difficult to do so with their standard accoutrements.

Formal Seating Plan for the Festive Board/Installation Banquet

If there is a top table, the Master is seated centrally; next to him on his right hand are:

Initiate;
Provincial Grand Master or his representative;
Grand Officers in descending order of seniority;
Senior guests.

And on his left hand are:

Immediate Past Master;
Chaplain;
Treasurer;
Secretary;
Director of Ceremonies;
Past Masters of the lodge in order of seniority.

The Wardens may be seated at the ends of the top table, or at the ends of the outermost sprig tables, depending on lodge custom and practice.

The Master's personal guests may be seated in front of him on an adjacent sprig table, so that he has the opportunity to converse with them during the meal.

If there is music or the Master's song to be sung during or after the meal, it is likely that the brethren involved will want to sit together, to make any last minute organisational arrangements, and the pianist will probably prefer to be seated near to the piano.

Some senior attendees, which may include Grand Officers (or Officers of Grand Lodge, but preferably not Grand Lodge Officers), may request to be seated elsewhere in the table plan, perhaps to be near other guests who cannot be placed adjacent to the top table for them to converse with. You might even invite them to consider doing this occasionally, so that they can mix with the other ranks of Masons present; it has a remarkably encouraging effect if junior brethren realise they are sitting and talking with senior brethren, and both can usefully learn informally from the others, which they might not otherwise be able to do if the seating plans always follow a strict hierarchical order.

Taking Wine and Formal Toasts at a Festive Board or Installation Banquet

Taking Wine

The taking of wine with the brethren can be fraught with difficulties. Too little will leave some attendees feeling overlooked, and too much of a good thing will potentially spoil the proceedings for everyone. It is unnecessary to interrupt every course of the meal by taking wine, so try to complete the necessary items in perhaps one or two sessions, and then the diners can continue their meals in peace.

The following list may be of assistance in selecting with whom the Master will take wine:

Wardens (particularly if they join in with the Master in subsequent toasts)**
Provincial Grand Master or representative (he may then take wine with everyone else)
Grand Officers
Provincial Grand Officers
Visiting Masters
A brother on a special celebration, e.g. 50th anniversary
Officers and members of the lodge who participated in the ceremony
Candidate (new Initiate, Fellowcraft, Master Mason)
Joining members
Master Elect
New lodge Officers
Personal guests
Other (or all) members of the lodge
Other (or all) visiting brethren
Any brother with whom he has not yet taken wine (an alternative catch-all)

**The Master, Immediate Past Master, or Director of Ceremonies may introduce this by using part of the long Tyler's toast along these lines:
Master — Brother Wardens, how do you report your respective stations?
Senior Warden — The glasses are fully charged in the West.
Junior Warden — The glasses are fully charged in the South.
Master — And I report the same for the East and North; Brother Wardens, I have much pleasure in taking wine with you both.

89

Toasts

The following is a generally accepted set of toasts to be used selectively on formal occasions:

Monarch (and the Craft)

M W Grand Master

R W Pro Grand Master
R W Deputy Grand Master
R W Assistant Grand Master
And the rest of the Grand Officers, present and past

R W Provincial Grand Master

Deputy Provincial Grand Master
Assistant Provincial Grand Master(s)
And the rest of the Provincial Grand Officers, present and past, of this and other Provinces, and holders of London Grand Rank

Master

Immediate Past (and Installing) Master

Installation team

The candidate (normally proposed by his proposer or seconder)

Masonic charities

Absent brethren (some lodges try to organise this to be taken at 9pm — when the hands of the clock are at the square — and this toast should if possible not be taken before the first two toasts, but if the meal is very late then it may have to be taken on the hour)

Founders of the lodge

Visiting brethren

Tyler's toast (may be the long version at an Installation, Olde English night or other special occasion)

If the lodge responds to the toasts using firing glasses, then there is usually no fire after absent brethren if it precedes the loyal toast, after Masonic charities, or after the Tyler's toast, or there may be 'silent fire'.

The charity collection, whether taken in the lodge room or at the festive board, may be announced when the total amount is known, possibly by the Master during his closing remarks.

Mastering the Ritual

When you become a Principal Officer your participation in the lodge ritual increases. The Assistant Officers all have short speaking parts, and the Deacons have some escorting duties to perform, but the chunks of ritual increase in size as you move further upwards. The Wardens may deliver the working tools of each degree, the charges in the three degrees, and the Senior Warden has the investiture of the aprons. The Master himself has not only several short passages in each of the degrees, but with the obligations and explanations there are many more sizeable chunks for him to tackle.

How do you cope with it all? You may be in a lodge which shares the work around juniors and Past Masters, which helps; or you may be in a lodge that expects all three degrees to be undertaken each year by one individual as well as the installation. If you are not a born ritualist, then where do you start? Each person will have adopted his own method but, as someone who has not found the ritual particularly easy to learn, I can pass on my ideas on a possible technique.

You might have heard of the question: 'How do you eat an elephant?' For a single person it can appear to be a mammoth (sorry) task, and impossible at one sitting for anyone. And indeed it is; the elephant will be eaten part by part each day over several weeks. And that is how you can succeed, even if you initially find the ritual awkward to recall. You read the first sentence of a passage several times and then try to repeat it without looking at the page; with a long sentence break it down line by line. Then you read the second sentence several times and do the same, and now you can try to recall the two sentences sequentially. You then tackle the third sentence, and so on.

By now your brain is beginning to remember that at the end of one sentence there is a trigger for the next sentence. If you encounter a list of items, it may help to recall that they are in alphabetical order or the reverse, and perhaps the first item becomes the key word for the sentence after which the rest of the list unfolds. You may find that you need to identify a key word in each sentence, preferably near the beginning, which can then become this trigger. Once you have absorbed one paragraph you can start on the next, and concentrate on this alone; at a later time you can try to run the two sections together. After a while the sentences in a paragraph begin to fall into line automatically, and then your brain is searching for the key words in the first sentences of each paragraph so that they too fall into sequence.

Some parts of the ritual seem particularly tortuous to remember, while other passages seem to flow much more easily. The explanation of the second degree tracing board is essentially a story, and many Masons find this style simpler to master, and the same applies to the traditional history in the third degree. Some parts of the ritual, such as the long second degree working tools and the Installation addresses to the Master, Wardens and brethren, seem to have been polished by our predecessors into memorable passages of English prose, but each will have his favourite sections of the ritual. Our ceremonies have been developed over several centuries and sometimes the wording from yesteryear is initially a little unusual but, once mastered, it can also be more memorable. To some people, for example, the wording in King James' Bible for Ecclesiastes 12, St John's Gospel 1, and 1 Corinthians 13 has never been surpassed by later versions of the same text.

One result that committing the ritual to memory achieves is that it makes you think about what you are saying. You may have heard it many times in lodge delivered by other people, but you will now have to assimilate the meaning of the different strings of words if you are going to recite them with any confidence as well as for the candidate to comprehend. You will begin to place emphasis on certain words and phrases, and thereby make the recitation more intelligible to the candidate and other attendees at the meeting, and indeed these various points of emphasis can become additional key words or phrases that your brain can identify with as it recalls the ritual.

If you are trying to learn the ritual on your own, it is important that you try to visualise that part of the ceremony you are delivering. In the world of sport, athletes are trained to visualise breaking the tape first, because if your mind has an image of you crossing the line in second place, then that is probably the best you will achieve in the actual race. So do not learn an obligation in one non-stop delivery; pause after each phrase so that the candidate has time to repeat what you have said, otherwise in the meeting the first words of the candidate will throw your recital off track. Go further than that, and visualise the events leading up to the obligation: the perambulations and the interactions with the Master and Wardens, the presentation of the candidate, his being taught how to approach the pedestal, the words prior to him repositioning himself at the pedestal. If you are presenting the working tools, you may visualise the end of the previous section of the ceremony, you making your way or being escorted to the Warden's pedestal, saluting the Master and picking up the tools, showing each of the tools at the appropriate moment and then replacing them on the pedestal, saluting the Master and returning to your seat. Then with any luck the actual meeting will run almost exactly parallel to your visualisation, and your presentation will be as perfect as in the privacy of your home or wherever you learned the ritual.

The rate at which you can commit all of these passages to memory will vary from person to person. Even the best ritualists will rarely admit that it was easy for them to learn any passage of prose, and many of us do not number ourselves with the best. But by taking some time and effort there have been countless brethren who have surprised themselves what they can remember once their brains have been exercised in this manner, and by hard work many perhaps initially less capable people have managed to acquit themselves very creditably. And no-one in Masonry should decry the honest endeavours of a brother in lodge, however limited the challenge he has undertaken and whether or not it was as impeccable as on the previous practice night, because for most people sincerity and an honest attempt will always outweigh word-perfection without feeling.

And this prompts another thought, that the lodge practice meeting is a good testing ground for what you are trying to learn, with everyone there willing you on as you move from section to section of your allotted task. The practice night has the other bonus, unrealised when you are learning the ritual alone, of having an audience present — and at the lodge meeting you will be performing for a key audience of the candidate as well as the other visitors present. Your lodge may have a formal Lodge of Instruction, but even if it does not, there may be one organised by another lodge nearby that you can attend if it helps. The caveat is that another lodge may not use your exact ritual for the movements around the lodge room for example, but if you are performing a discrete section of the ceremony there is a good chance that the words will be standard for most lodges, and it will still provide a useful practice ground for you. The main decision is to plan ahead, take a realistic appraisal of your current capabilities, and begin the learning process with enough time to complete it well before the lodge meeting in which you have to deliver the finished article. The adage 'practice makes perfect' is as true for Masonic ritual as for anything else, and with enough dedication you will be pleasantly surprised by what you can achieve — good luck in your endeavours!

Further Reading

Further Reading – there are many books and papers that go into more detail about topics necessarily covered very briefly in this book. There are some references to the offices of Warden and Master in the Prestonian lectures, published under the auspices of Ars Quattuor Coronati (AQC). The office of Warden has been discussed in a Prestonian lecture about Deacons:

1985: Sinclair Bruce, *'…not only Ancient but useful and necessary Officers…the Deacons.'*
For the Master there have been several papers, including:
1977: Harry Carr, *'The Evolution of the Installation Ceremony and Ritual.'*
1997: Nevill Barker Cryer, *'The Master's Part: a Re-appraisal.'*
For wider reading there are sections within the following books:
1973 (2nd Edition): E H Cartwright, *'A Commentary on the Freemasonic Ritual.'*
1973: Bernard E Jones, *'Freemasons' Guide and Compendium.'*
1983: Colin Dyer, *'Symbolism in Craft Freemasonry.'*

Another method of learning more about the principal offices is to peruse the different versions of the Craft ritual, as the variations can sometimes serve to add a further nuance or interpretation to your current view of the ritual. Lewis Masonic publishes a wide range of rituals that are different from the standard Emulation version, and they include Logic, Oxford, Sussex, Taylor's, Universal and the West End workings. These and other books for freemasons are available from Lewis Masonic Mail Order Dept, 4 Watling Drive, Hinckley, Leics LE10 3EY; request a catalogue by mail or telephone (01455 254450).

Acknowledgements

I would like to thank those members of the Brigantes' Ritual Working Party who assisted in the proof reading and commented on the draft of this book; and a special thanks to James Abbott of Brigantes Lodge 9734, Tim Smith of Gild of St Mary Lodge 7288, Roy Willis of Cestrian Lodge 425, and Jack Kielty of Lodge of St John 191, and other lodges for providing/allowing photographs of their lodge furniture; as well as placing on record — as ever — the patience of my wife Linda while I was immersed in researching for and compiling this book.